Disco

DISCOVERING GOD'S WILL

SINCLAIR B. FERGUSON

THE BANNER OF TRUTH TRUST

THE BANNER OF TRUTH TRUST
3 Murrayfield Road, Edinburgh EH12 6EL
P.O. Box 621, Carlisle, Pennsylvania, 17013, U.S.A.

*

The Banner of Truth Trust 1981
ISBN 0 85151 334 4

*

Filmset, printed and bound in Great Britain by
Hazell Watson & Viney Ltd, Aylesbury, Bucks

TO
DR TOM MURRAY
Missionary in China
General Practitioner in Glasgow
Elder in St George's-Tron
Friend
Who gave me early guidance
in the way of Christ

Contents

Introduction

ARE you in need of guidance? Most Christians believe that God is the Guide of their lives. In fact it is difficult to imagine a Christian who does not believe that. From earliest years, perhaps, you have been able to say: 'The Lord is my shepherd . . . He leads me . . .' (Ps. 23:1-2). Certainly during your Christian life, if you are a Christian, there have been many situations in which you have turned to the Lord and said: 'I do not know what to do here, help me!' You have proved his guiding hand in the large and small affairs of life. Yes, you need guidance. Yes, God has promised to be your Guide. Yes, God has undoubtedly guided you already.

So far, so good! But we know that things are not always so straightforward. Sometimes we are very deeply perplexed. We do not know what to do, or which of two alternative courses of action to pursue. We need guidance from God very much indeed. *But how does God guide us?* How do we come to recognise what his will is?

We are not far along the Christian pathway before these or similar questions begin to puzzle many of us. Instead of thinking about the wonder of guidance, we begin to feel perplexed and uncertain. We look back on the 'honeymoon' period of our Christian experience, and we realise that in a gracious, fatherly way, God was smoothing much of the road for us. He was helping us to take the baby steps of our Christian life in a guarded atmosphere. 'He gathers the lambs in his arms and carries them close to his heart' (Is. 40:11). We were too young then to realise all the pitfalls and problems there might be. Now we are older in the faith, perhaps a little wiser and humbler, but probably also a little more complicated and even confused. We still believe that God guides us. But, the niggling question remains: *How does God guide us?*

The Christian who lives in the last quarter of the twentieth century is probably faced with more answers to his questions than any previous generation of his fellow-believers. There have never been so many different views of the way in which God leads us as there are today. Writers, preachers, Christian leaders, friends, all offer advice – yes, even guidance – about guidance!

The world in which we live brings its pressures to bear upon our thinking. Silently it sets standards which we unconsciously adopt. Insistently it erodes the principles of true spiritual guidance exemplified in the pages of Scripture, and blinds us with its own dazzling array of wisdom. But it was in the wisdom of this world that men crucified Christ. That same wisdom applied to our lives will crucify afresh the Lord of glory (Heb. 6:6).

The spirit of the age in which we live also offers its guidance to us. It is hungry for immediate, short-term results. It is impatient. It cannot see life in the long-term because it looks at life without the perspective of eternal realities. Its guidance will gain us the world in which we live. But since in the process of gaining it we shall lose our souls, where is the profit?

Then, even *the church* may fail us. It can offer us more alternatives about guidance than the world does!

It may spread before us guidance by intuition, guidance by dreams, guidance by visions, guidance by prophecies, guidance by tongues, guidance by peer-groups, guidance by leaders – and so on, in an apparently never-ending stream of possibilities. We can take one emphasis seriously, and perhaps make shipwreck of our souls. Or, we can bounce from one to another until confusion brings us to a halt. Nowhere are the words of the hymn quite so apt: 'And guide us when perplexed'. The trouble is that *it is about guidance that so many Christians are perplexed!*

Against this background he would be a bold man who thought he could offer the last word to his fellow-Christians on the subject of guidance. This book is very far from being the last word! But it emphasises certain things which may be of special help at this particular time of the church's life.

In the first place, we need to recognise that we do not find God's guidance for our lives by reading a book on guidance! All that a book on guidance can do for us is to underscore the ways in which God has promised to reveal his purposes to his people, and the principles which he characteristically employs to guide them. As will become clear in the pages which follow, *there is no avoiding, and no substitute for, the sometimes long, arduous experience of discovering the will of God in our own lives*. There is all the difference in the world between knowing how this will take place and it actually taking place in personal experience.

In the second place, I have tried to focus attention on issues in the biblical teaching about guidance which constantly arise in the lives of Christians. It seems to be statistically true that most Christians made their first profession of Christ when they were younger rather than older. The discovery of the Christian life and the ways of God consequently run parallel to many of the fundamental discoveries we make about ourselves and life in general.

There are three particular areas in which we form patterns of life which largely determine the whole course of life. We form patterns of behaviour – a lifestyle. We decide which occupation and career we will pursue. We decide to marry or not to marry. To each of these areas of vital concern, I have devoted a chapter. You will not find definite answers in these pages to such questions as: Should Christians drink alcohol? Should I marry Wendy or Jenny? Should I become an accountant or a teacher? But you will find principles which, when conscientiously applied to your own circumstances, will keep you in the pathway along which God's will may be discovered. To that extent I have tried to deal with practical issues.

In the third place, I have tried to convey that we learn about guidance primarily by learning about *the Guide*. It is the knowledge of God and his ways with men which ultimately gives us stability in doing his will.

Think of how this was true of many of the saints in the Old Testament Scriptures. Job is an example. He was in great difficulty. His heart was broken with sorrow and pain. He desperately needed guidance to know what God was doing in his life. He received advice from the finest theologians of his day; men who (for all their faults) had sufficient compassion to sit with him in silence for many days (Job 2:13). But through his time of trial he needed more than knowledge *about* God. He needed *to know God himself*. That was, ultimately, what God gave him. Before, his ears had heard of God; now he had seen God and come to know him (Job 42:5).

There is no escaping this great principle. That is why Martin Luther said that true Christianity consists in personal pronouns. For guidance, the knowledge of the Lord's will, is *not* the ability to say that God is a Shepherd, Supplier, Guide, Leader and Restorer. It *is* the ability to say:

> The Lord is *my* Shepherd, *I* shall lack nothing.
> He makes *me* lie down in green pastures,
> he leads *me* beside quiet waters,
> he restores *my* soul.
> He guides *me* in paths of righteousness
> for his name's sake.

My prayer is that through these pages you may receive some help and clarification about how God will guide you and perhaps grant illumination on the very areas of your life which perplex you at the moment. But most of all I pray that you will discover afresh the gracious ways of God, and God himself as your Guide.

SINCLAIR B. FERGUSON
Glasgow, 1981

1: *God's Ultimate Purpose*

GOD is the Shepherd of his people. He leads them (Ps. 23:1). He sent his Son to lead them (Jn. 10:3). As Christians we are assured in a multitude of ways that he will guide us, and keep us. That is the task of the shepherd. It is a task which God himself has undertaken because of his great love for his people.

The assurance of God's guidance is one of the characteristics of the Christian. It marks him out from his fellow men. Why should this be so? Because the very idea that God guides us implies that we live according to the *path* which he has laid down, that our lives have a *purpose* in the present, as well as a *destiny* for the future. As a result many young converts are struck by the fact that, whereas before they wandered aimlessly through life, now it is full of direction and significance.

In biblical times this was a revolutionary thought to the people who first heard the gospel and the call of God. When God spoke to Abraham, made his covenant with him, and assured him of his great and glorious purposes for the future, the experience not only transformed his own life, it injected a new way of looking at life into his world.

When the gospel spread throughout the world of the New Testament, dominated as it was by Greek ways of thinking, something equally remarkable began to happen. The long-accepted idea that history in general, and life in particular, was cyclical – that is, that life really did go round in circles – was abolished. Christ began to straighten out men's view of history.

When Paul spoke to the philosophers of Athens about the end of the world and the judgment of God, he was saying that life had a beginning, a direction, and a climax in judgment. The history of mankind (and our personal history too) is not cyclical. It has direction.

We could be forgiven for thinking this is just an abstruse and somewhat academic point. But, look around you. The perspective on life of your contemporaries is very similar to that of those ancient Greeks. Life for them is little more than a round of activities in which they seek whatever satisfaction they can find. The average man does not rack his brains to ask whether life has any ultimate significance. He has accepted the idea that life is without final purpose, and so he naturally devotes himself to whatever interests him at the moment. By contrast the Christian seems almost like a creature from another world, from another time scale altogether. As we will see, that is precisely what he has become! He walks on the *path* which God has laid; he enjoys the *purpose* for his life which God has ordained; he looks forward to the *destiny* which God has planned.

Let us examine these three features of the Christian life. We will do so in reverse order, and discover in the process that each of them has a direct bearing on the guidance of God.

The Destiny God has Planned

Why has God made me? What is my life for? Jesus answered these questions in one of the most poignant hours of his life. When he prayed for his disciples, and all those who would believe in him through their witness, he said:

> Father, I want those you have given me to be with me where I am, and to see my glory, the glory you have given me because you loved me before the creation of the world.[1]

Jn. 17:24

Simply expressed, our Lord recognised that God has a plan for his people ('those you have given me'). Jesus asked that the purpose of his death for us may be fulfilled in us – that we may see the glory of God, and live in his presence. God, his glory and his presence form the destiny of the Christian.

This is why the Bible pictures the life of faith as a life of pilgrimage. The perspective of the believer throughout biblical times was forward looking. He was going somewhere, expecting something in the future. The epitome of unbelief is consequently illustrated in Lot's wife. Warned to flee from the cities which God would destroy, she *looked back* (Gen. 19:26). By contrast, the heroes of the faith listed in Hebrews 11 are, without exception, characterised by anticipation, hope and expectation for the future (see Heb. 11:13 particularly). Because we have a destiny, we become pilgrims. We are making what John Bunyan so brilliantly described as: *The Pilgrim's Progress from this world to that which is to come.*

The New Testament explicitly tells us that we are pilgrims. The idea seems to have been a favourite one of the apostle Peter. He refers to the recipients of his first letter as 'strangers in the world' (1 Pet. 1:1) and as 'aliens and strangers in the world' (1 Pet. 2:11). The

[1] Unless otherwise indicated all biblical quotations are from *The New International Version*, © 1978 The New York International Bible Society.

point he is making is that our residence here is temporary. We do not really belong to this age. *The inference he draws is that our life-style should not be determined by this age.* Paul makes a similar point when he complains to the Corinthians that they are living like ordinary men. But the Christian is not an ordinary man! (1 Cor. 3:3 R.S.V.) He is a stranger. He takes the determining influences on his life from another world altogether. It is not at all surprising that this world finds him strange and difficult to understand (1 Pet. 4:4).

The child of God is a citizen of another world. He has 'another king, one called Jesus' (Acts 17:7). His commonwealth, says Paul, is not here on the earth, but in heaven (Phil. 3:20). He is an ambassador from the Lord Jesus (2 Cor. 5:20). His life is intended to be a miniature court of his king. His call to go home to his own commonwealth will one day come. But meanwhile he is establishing his life according to heavenly, rather than earthly principles. He has set his heart on the things that are above, where Christ is seated at the right hand of God (Col. 3:1). No wonder he is different!

Do you notice, in passing, that this elementary principle of the life of faith immediately solves some of the problems which many Christians have? How many times have we asked (or heard others ask): Is the Christian allowed to do this, or that? Sometimes, in response, we build for ourselves a tall list of rules and regulations, 'do's and don'ts'. We then hedge these around and make them the determining factors in our judgments of the quality of life other Christians lead. All the time, like Pharisees (who were originally the holiness movement of the Old Testament church) we are missing the point, straining out gnats and swallowing camels (cf. Matt. 23:24).

The principle that the Christian is a pilgrim with a destiny will solve many of these problems at a stroke. When he sets his mind on establishing a life patterned on heaven, many of these issues become irrelevant, because his life is being lived on a different plane altogether. He will not need to judge that some action is morally wrong. It may not necessarily be so. But in the life which aims to move out of the pollution of the world's atmosphere, he will discover that many of these indifferent issues become precisely that to him: matters of indifference.

The Purpose God has Ordained

Sometimes I think the only question in the famous *Shorter Catechism* most of us know is the first one. But if there is any question which will help us to live the Christian life, it is indeed this:

> *What is the chief end of man?* Man's chief end is to glorify God, and to enjoy him for ever.

These words are profoundly biblical; much more biblical and Christian than many of us recognise. For we moderns tend to think of the Bible in two distinct halves: the Old Testament which tells us about the glory of God, and the New Testament which reveals the wonder of his love. But the New Testament itself teaches us that the chief end of the love of God and the work of Christ is *to promote God's glory*. All that Christ did during his ministry had this motivation (Jn. 12:28; 14:13; 17:1, 4). The essence of the Christian life is that God should be glorified in us. The aim of our evangelism is 'so that the grace which is reaching more and more people may cause thanksgiving to overflow to the glory of God' (2 Cor. 4:15).

This is something which the apostle Paul expounds

19

at considerable length in his writings. The whole concept of our salvation, as he works it out in Romans, is set against the background that 'all have sinned and *fall short of the glory of God.*' Salvation is not only the process by which God restores us to the hope of his glory (Rom. 5:2); it is also (and fundamentally) the way in which God restores his own glory, and enhances it through his amazing grace. In Ephesians Paul gives a more detailed description of the various movements in the symphony of salvation. In each of them the recurring motif is: *to the praise of the glory of God* (Eph. 1:6, 12, 13). Election, redemption, adoption – all contribute to this great theme.

The glory of God is a determining factor in the Christian's life, or ought to be. We are being changed from one degree of glory to another (2 Cor. 3:18). Consequently examples like Abraham are set before us. He 'was strengthened in his faith and gave glory to God' by believing God's promise (Rom. 4:20). The purpose of our obedience and fruitfulness is always to bring glory to our Father (Matt. 5:16; Jn. 15:8). When we have differences of opinion about a course of action, the decisive factor is to be 'what tends most to the glory of God?' (1 Cor. 10:31).

There is, in fact, no more basic question for us to ask than this: *Will this course of action tend to further the glory of God?* How we know what will tend to the glory of God is recorded in the second question of the Shorter Catechism, and we shall consider it more fully later. But for the moment we need to press more heavily on this general question. Is this the star by which we set the course of our lives? Is the glory of God the driving principle of our actions? God will not separate the guidance he gives us in his word, or the way in which he governs our circumstances, from his settled purpose of gaining glory for his Son in our lives. If we do not seek his glory, we cannot be walking in the way of his blessing. If we seek his glory, then we can be sure that we shall discover his light shed on our paths.

There is a key to our thinking about the glory of God. What does it mean that our lives should reflect his glory? It means *likeness to Jesus*. The fact that God has set us apart for the praise of the glory of his grace (Eph. 1:3–6) is further explained by Paul. He says that God's loving predestining of our lives intends us, 'to be conformed to the image of his Son, that he might be the firstborn among many brothers' (Rom. 8:29). To live for the glory of God means to imitate Jesus. It means to become familiar with the inner springs which activated all his behaviour, and to put these principles into practice in our own lives. It means to live in dependence on the Holy Spirit who has been given to us with the specific function of bringing glory to Jesus in our lives (Jn. 16:14). According to Ephesians 4:20–24, it means to live in righteousness and holiness.

Do you deliberately seek to imitate Jesus? Perhaps you were brought up on the mistaken notion that the imitation of Christ was the way of salvation. Now you know that this is not the case. Only through faith in Christ, as a crucified Saviour and a risen and reigning Lord, can we ever find salvation. In your discovery of this you have reacted against the idea that being a Christian is living a life which imitates the principles of his life. But that too would be a mistake. For we receive Christ Jesus as Saviour in order to follow him as our Lord and Example: 'I have set you an example' he said, 'that you should do as I have done for you' (Jn. 13:15). Paul says we should not please ourselves. Why not? 'Christ did not please himself' (Rom. 15:3).

Therefore, 'Your attitude should be the same as that of Christ Jesus' (Phil. 2:5).

This is the sure way to promote the glory of God. It is the sure way to walk worthy of your calling to be a pilgrim:

> *May the mind of Christ my Saviour*
> *Live in me from day to day,*
> *By His love and power controlling*
> *All I do and say.*

Katie Barclay Wilkinson

Is your life governed by a heavenly purpose which sheds beams of glory upon the way you live now? Is the glory of God *your* chief end? Do you hold Jesus Christ before your eyes as the Guide and Example by which you will live? It is as we thus follow Jesus Christ that we are enabled to glorify his God and Father (Rom. 15:5, 6).

The Path God has Laid

God means to guide our lives so that they may reflect the glory of his Son. In order to accomplish this he calls us to be imitators of Christ. But his ultimate purposes require more than our response. They necessitate his personal action in working out his plan. He makes us like Christ. When we stand before him in his glory, we shall be like Christ (1 Jn. 3:2). But in order to make us like Christ *then*, our Father has already begun to make us like Christ *now*. The pattern he uses in the Christian's life is precisely the pattern he employed in the life of his obedient Son Jesus.

What is this pattern? When we look at the life of Jesus in the Gospels, and reflect on its significance through the teaching of the apostles in the rest of the New Testament, a very clear pattern emerges. Jesus was called to leave aside his glory by taking the form of a servant (Phil. 2:7). In whatever way he became conscious of the will of God in his life, he certainly learned that his mission was to be the Servant of the Lord whom Isaiah had prophesied. Time and again this pattern is worked out in the Gospels until it reaches its climax in his passion. Christ humbled himself under the mighty hand of God, and was in due season exalted (1 Pet. 5:6). He suffered and *then* entered glory (Lk. 24:26). He endured the cross and despised the shame in order that he might experience the joy which was set before him (Heb. 12:2). The shape of his life was the pattern of the cross.

We can never repeat too often to one another that this remains the pattern of God's will and purpose in our lives. He did not break the mould of his plan when Christ ascended. On the contrary, the *raison d'être* of Christ's work was that he might bring many other sons to glory (Heb. 2:10). He himself grew into complete manhood and lived wholly in the will of God through suffering. The work of bringing many sons to glory involves repeating that process in their lives too.

In practical terms this familiarity with the way in which God works will bring enormous stability to our lives. It will make it possible for us to trust the purposes of God for us, even when they seem to be most painful. We will learn thus the paradox of the Christian life: it is a path to glory, through tribulations (Acts 14:22). The way in which God leads us is the way of following Christ in bearing the cross. Any 'guidance' which contradicts this principle will lack the familiar autograph of Christ. Any 'voice' which beckons us to forsake this pathway we will silence. For we

23

will have come to recognise the accents of our Master. There is no voice like the voice of the One who has been crucified.

So, when we come to Christ and ask: 'Will you be my Shepherd and my Guide through life?' he asks in return: 'Will you take up the cross daily, and follow me?' The two things can never be separated: Christ-likeness *then*, in glory, must be preceded by Christ-likeness *now*, under the cross. By it the world has been crucified to us. By it we are also crucified to the world (Gal. 6:14).

> *My goal is God Himself, not joy, nor peace,*
> *Nor even blessing, but Himself, my God;*
> *'Tis His to lead me there – not mine, but His –*
> *At any cost, dear Lord, by any road.*
>
> *So faith bounds forward to its goal in God,*
> *And love can trust her Lord to lead her there;*
> *Upheld by Him, my soul is following hard*
> *Till God hath full fulfilled my deepest prayer.*
>
> *No matter if the way be sometimes dark,*
> *No matter though the cost be oft-times great,*
> *He knoweth how I best shall reach the mark;*
> *The way that leads to Him must needs be strait.*
>
> *One thing I know, I cannot say Him nay;*
> *One thing I do, I press towards my Lord;*
> *My God, my glory here, from day to day,*
> *And in the glory there my great Reward.*

F. Brook

Is that really our ambition? Do you really want this

kind of divine guidance? Have you counted the cost?
Will you deny self, take up the cross, and follow Christ
into his perfect will for your life?

> Lord Crucified, O mark Thy holy cross
> On motive, preference, all fond desires;
> On that which self in any form inspires
> Set Thou that sign of loss.
> And when the touch of death is here and there
> Laid on a thing most precious in our eyes,
> Let us not wonder, let us recognise
> The answer to this prayer.

Amy Carmichael

Is that the kind of guidance you seek?

2: Guidelines for Guidance

T H E purpose of these chapters is to give instruction in God's will. They provide a summary of the kind of teaching you would receive over a much longer period of time, and probably in a less systematic way, listening to regular biblical exposition.

There is a good deal to be said for learning scriptural principles in *that* way, over an extended period of time. There is also a very good reason for receiving it through preaching rather than through the more systematic statement of a book on guidance. The slower, spoken, less systematic method of learning guards us against the illusion that God's will can be learned overnight.

Yet, it may also be helpful to gather biblical instruction together like this. For in a systematic treatment we can at least begin to grasp hold of the great principles. We may find some of our questions answered, and some of the issues which concern us clarified. We might be reluctant to ask a minister or Christian friend to devote the considerable length of time it would probably take to talk these matters through to the end. The aim of this book is to be a servant of whatever teaching and pastoral instruction you already receive, not a substitute for it.

It is important for us to return to the question which we raised in the middle of chapter one. There we saw that the ultimate purpose behind all God's guidance is the promotion of his glory. According to the Shorter

Catechism (following Scripture), this is our chief end. But, we hinted, a new question arises in this context: How do we know what tends to the glory of God? *That is precisely the subject of the Catechism's second question:*

What rule hath God given to direct us how we may glorify and enjoy him? The word of God, which is contained in the scriptures of the Old and New Testaments, is the only rule to direct us how we may glorify and enjoy him.

Have you ever recognised what a radical, all-embracing principle that is? There can be little doubt that it is here that the many differences Christians have about guidance begin to emerge. In fact it is possible for Christians to subscribe together to the authority, infallibility and reliability of God's word – yet, at the same time, differ strongly here, and to accept radically different views of how God guides us. If there is one critical issue we must face about divine guidance it is this one. Is Scripture our guide? Is Scripture ultimately 'the *only* rule to direct us how we may glorify' God?

What does this mean in practical terms? Obviously it indicates that many of the modes of guidance which are held up to us today are to be examined with much more care than they sometimes are. Whenever the suggestion is made that 'the Lord has led me to do this', the question has to be asked: Am I doing this in obedience to, and consistently with, the one rule for guidance given to me in Scripture?

It may be objected that to say Scripture is our only rule is itself an unscriptural statement. After all, in Scripture we have direct voices from God, visions, prophecies, and other means by which God communicated his will to men. That is quite true. It seems that at one time God's people decided difficult issues on the basis of lots. They probably used the two precious stones in the High Priest's breastplate for this (see Ex. 28:30; Numb. 27:21). If he drew Urim out, the answer might be 'Yes'; if Thummim, then the answer might be 'No, God does not want you to pursue this course of action'. So Proverbs 16:33 tells us, 'The lot is cast into the lap, but its decision is from the Lord'. In the New Testament we find that the replacement for Judas Iscariot was chosen by lots cast by the rest of the apostles (Acts 1:15–26). But Christian churches today do not resort to lots in order to know God's will. Why not? Because we recognise that these things belonged to the infancy of the church of God, and not to the new age of the gospel and the full enjoyment of the Spirit of sonship (See Gal. 4:1–7). We recognise that God has spoken in *various* ways. Now he has spoken *finally* in his Son Jesus (Heb. 1:1–2). The implication, which the book of Hebrews works out at considerable length, is that we no longer live in the age in which God reveals his will to us in these diverse ways. Now he has perfectly revealed his will to us in Jesus, and we will find his guidance enshrined in the pages of our only witness to Christ – the Holy Scriptures.

In a sense the same point had been made centuries before, at least in principle. For Psalm 19 tells us of the way in which God can be known through the autograph he has left on the created order. But this is contrasted with the clear revelation God has given in his word. The heavens declare *his glory*; but if we wish to know *his will*, we must turn to his word. It was this truth which Isaac Watts so beautifully captured when he wrote:

> *The heavens declare Thy glory, Lord,*
> *In every star Thy wisdom shines;*

But when our eyes behold Thy Word,
We read Thy Name in fairer lines.

There is *progress* in revelation. As one epoch passes away, God introduces a new way of communicating with men. Now that we live in what the New Testament calls the 'last days', his final way of communicating with men has been deposited with us. Indeed, the New Testament speaks about this 'deposit' (*paradosis* = 'tradition' in A.V.). We are to hold to it (2 Thess. 2:15; 3:6). There is now no other rule than the one we find enshrined in the word of God which Christ has given to his people through the authority of apostolic ministry.

How then does God make his will known to us? Primarily by teaching us about himself and our relationship to him. John Calvin expressed it perfectly when he wrote at the beginning of his greatest book:

> Nearly all the wisdom we possess, that is to say, true and sound wisdom, consists of two parts: the knowledge of God and of ourselves.[1]

As we come to know the character of God, and his ways with men, we shall increasingly discover this wisdom – that is, the practical knowledge of his will and the ways in which it is to be put into action.

Scripture provides this knowledge for us basically in three ways:

1. God gives direct *commandments and prohibitions* to us. Automatically we will think of the Ten Commandments. Here are principles which govern life in all places at all times. Because they are the expression of God's original purposes for man, they stand throughout

[1] John Calvin, *Institutes of the Christian Religion*, trans. F. L. Battles, ed. J. T. McNeill, 1960, I.i.1.

29

all the epochs of the kingdom of God. There are certain applications of them which applied only during the period of the *Mosaic* Law. But the laws, the principles themselves stand for ever.

There are also other commands. There are apostolic commands in every one of the New Testament letters. When we say we believe in the Apostolic Church, one of the things we mean is that, in a sense, we are still under apostolic authority. There are still apostles today – they are in the church triumphant – but they continue to exercise their Christ-ordained ministry through the pages of Scripture and the commands they have given to us. Then there are the commands of Jesus; the applications he made of God's word, for example in the Sermon on the Mount. The whole Bible is full of clear-cut guidance to help us to live to the glory of God!

2. There are *principles* worked out in Scripture. It would be a mistake, for example, to think that becoming a Christian always meant that we had to sell all that we have and give the proceeds to the poor – as our Lord told one young man. But, none the less, there is a principle enshrined in Jesus' command. It is the principle that Jesus must be Lord of all, or he is not Lord at all. What he said to the young ruler was simply a special application which revealed that the young man had not really responded to that principle in his heart (cf. Matt. 19:16–30).

3. There are also *illustrations*; biographical accounts which demonstrate how these general principles of God's dealings with his people work out in personal experience and practice. They are recorded in the third person, but sometimes (in the Psalms and elsewhere) poignantly described in the first person. They show

the ways of God with men, and teach what God requires of us, does for us, and works out through us.

How then does the Lord generally guide us through the rule of Scripture? Often when we are very young Christians, God seems to carry us along (Is. 40:11). We do not yet have the understanding to distinguish right from wrong, good from bad, better from best. We take what is set before us. We are children, and are only beginning to develop a sense of what the Lord's will is.

But when we begin to grow, our heavenly Father begins to let us stand on our feet. We begin to take our first independent steps (*but not, of course, in an independent spirit*). We find that there are choices to make; we find that now we have to apply God's word to our own situation. *The chief need we have, therefore, is that of increased familiarity with and sensitivity to the wisdom of his word.*

The wonderful thing about God is that he is unchanging. His word is secure. He does not alter his mind. When we come to know him, his ways and his commands in Scripture, we can be sure that these hold good *always*. As we familiarise ourselves with all that he has revealed about himself, we learn to know his mind. As we grow in love for him we learn to be sensitive to how he will be thinking about our situation. As we grow more and more like him, we shall find that the yoke of Christ is comfortable on our shoulders. An instinct is created within us by which we know the will of the Lord for our lives. I have never found better words to express this notion than those of John Newton:

But how then may the Lord's guidance be expected? . . . In general, he guides and directs his people, by affording them, in answer to prayer, the light of his Holy Spirit, which enables them to understand and to love the Scriptures. The word of God is not to be used as a lottery; nor is it designed to instruct us by shreds and scraps, which, detached from their proper places, have no determinate import; but it is to furnish us with just principles, right apprehensions to regulate our judgements and affections, and thereby influence and direct our conduct.[1]

It may be said, by way of objection that this tends to lock God up in the pages of a book, and deny us any direct access to him and his will for our lives. Naturally, unless we maintain a real spirit of dependence upon the ministry of the Spirit leading us into the true meaning and application of Scripture, this may happen. But the abuse of a true principle is not really an argument against it. The principle itself must be allowed to stand. This is not to deny that we need supernatural aid to know the will of God. *On the contrary, this is exactly what is being affirmed!* But what we need supernatural help to do is to understand and apply our only rule of life, our only source of the knowledge of God and his will – the Holy Scriptures.

Does this not deny the many mysterious elements which so many Christians have discovered in the way God has led them? Not necessarily! There are several things we should notice.

There *is* much that is mysterious about the way God guides us. What is plain to him is frequently obscure to us. *But we are not called by God to make the mysterious, the unusual, the inexplicable the rule of our lives, but his word.* Further, it should be noted that very often these experiences, in which we begin to sense or understand what God's will for us is, fit in perfectly with the conviction that the word of God is a living, active guide to us. It penetrates between soul and spirit (Heb.

[1] *Letters of John Newton* (Banner of Truth edition), 1960, pp. 81–2.

4:12–13). We should not be surprised to discover that God brings special pressures to bear even on our subconscious thoughts by its deep application to the whole of our lives.[1]

There is an arresting example of this in Acts 16:6–10. Twice, by circumstances or through unknown causes, the Spirit of God prevented the apostle Paul and his companions from fulfilling their own plans. Then, one night, Paul had a vision. A man from Macedonia was begging him to come to that land. What did the little group of evangelists do? They 'got ready at once to leave' (Acts 16:10). Why? Because they concluded that God had called them. The verb Luke uses is interesting. It means to put two things together, side by side, in order to reach a conclusion. What these men did was not simply to obey the vision. They knew that no vision could be a rule of conduct. No; they placed the vision alongside all that they knew of God and all that he had been doing in their circumstances. Then they concluded that going to Macedonia would be consistent with all the light God had previously given about his present will for them. So they responded to the vision; not because it was a vision, but because of what they were able to conclude when they placed it alongside their knowledge of God. That prior knowledge was a combination of Old Testament Scripture and apostolic teaching. We too have that same combination. It is found in the pages of Holy Scripture.

Since this is the fundamental way in which God guides us, there will obviously be a number of other principles which will accompany the study of God's word. Three may be mentioned here.

Firstly, God's guidance will require patience on our

---

[1] See the excellent comments by John Murray, *Collected Writings*, vol. 1, 1976, p. 188.

part. His leading is not usually a direct assurance, a revelation, but his sovereign controlling of the circumstances of our lives, with the word of God as our rule. It is therefore inevitable that the unfolding of his purposes will take time – sometimes a very long time.

James makes an illuminating comment on this. He tells us how Job exhibited patience and perseverance under difficult circumstances. James compares Job's viewpoint with that of his own readers. Job did not know what God's ultimate purpose was. But the readers, hundreds of years later, do know, since they 'have seen what the Lord finally brought about' (Jas. 5:10–11). This contrast underlines the difficulties in which we often find ourselves. We do not see what the Lord will finally bring about. We sometimes think we have learned what his ultimate purpose is for our lives, only to discover that we are like climbers who thought the next peak was the final summit. Only when we reach it do we discover that there is still some further height to scale in the purposes of God.

I have sometimes thought that there are few more testing experiences than that of walking according to the light which God has given, only to discover that everything seems to be crumbling to dust in one's hands. Then there may come days of doubt, disillusionment with oneself, perhaps a tinge of bitterness, like that the psalmists sometimes record. Much later on we may be in a position to see how all the pieces of the jig-saw puzzle have fitted perfectly together. We can say 'Hitherto has the Lord helped us' (1 Sam. 7:12). But how we need patience, and how impatient we often are! Those who would submit to the guidance of God will need to pray for patience.

Secondly, it is essential that we come to see the part which our own thinking should play in the discernment

of the will of God. Indeed, it is an invaluable exercise
to reflect on the last phrase of that previous sentence.
It expresses a whole theology of guidance. Do you
speak about God's guidance as 'discerning the will of
God'? Or, do you usually speak of it in terms such as
'I felt led to do it'? Guidance, knowing God's will for
our lives, is *much more a matter of thinking than of
feeling*. We are not to be 'foolish' (literally 'mindless')
says Paul, but to *understand* what the will of the Lord
is (Eph. 5:17). Of course this is a spiritual matter. But
it is not merely a matter of spiritual sensitivity. It is
also a matter of *understanding*.

Psalm 119:66 teaches us to pray: 'Teach me knowledge and good judgment, for I believe in your commands'. This is precisely the balance we need to learn.
The psalmist uses the word '*taam*' which means 'taste'.
He is asking for such an understanding and thoughtful
application of God's word in his life that he will be
able, as occasion arises, to put his finger on the
direction which God wants him to take. This does not
come by experience alone. It comes through a combination of the study of God's word (where we learn the
great principles of his will), a heart which is submitted
to the Lord of the word, and the help of the Spirit who
illuminates the word and leads us into a true application
of its principles *to our own situation*. One of the
consequences of this is that we have a growing 'taste',
or sense, of the will of God. We no longer leaf through
Scripture in a flurry wondering whether there is some
word from God which will leap out of the pages to help
and inspire us! On the contrary, we will enjoy what the
apostle John called 'an anointing from the Holy One'
(1 Jn. 2:20). We will know God's will, because we can
'judge' or 'taste' the flavour of his purposes for us.

Knowing God's will is a matter of judgment. That is

why it is not an unspiritual practice, when faced with alternative ways of proceeding, to set down the pros and cons of the situation; the reasons, possibilities, problems of one decision in contrast with another. When we begin to evaluate these against a background of a general knowledge of the Lord's will in Scripture, we often find our minds drawn in a particular direction. As time passes we begin to feel the weight of one course of action rather than another.

Thirdly, the discovery of God's will and its accomplishment involves our *will*. I remember discussing my own future with a friend when I was considerably younger, and expressing doubts about my suitability for a particular sphere of labour. His response was illuminating: 'It is not lack of ability that is the issue here' he said, 'but the lack of the will to commit yourself to it.' That is the heart of the matter for many of us. 'Should I or shouldn't I?' is often, ultimately, a question of *'Will I, or will I not'*. It involves commitment and obedience as well as knowledge and understanding. Very often when young people say they are having problems about *guidance*, what they are really faced with is a problem about *obedience*. The issue at stake is whether we will walk along the paths of righteousness in which God will lead us. Are we willing to go through valleys of deep darkness, so long as he is with us?

Such is the point of Paul's great summons to consecration in Romans 12:1-2, where he begins radically to apply the many mercies of God about which he has been speaking in the previous chapters. Only consecration to Christ as a living, bodily sacrifice, will ever bring us to discover in experience that the will of God is 'good, pleasing and perfect'.

Perhaps this is why our forefathers rarely wrote or spoke about the problem of guidance. They had analysed the facts more biblically. They concentrated on teaching themselves and others the will of God which they discovered in Scripture, and the life of obedience to God in a daily submission to and application of his truth.

For some the way ahead may seem very clear, and straight. For others the position may seem to be the very reverse. For some, the great issues of guidance may be settled, apparently, in a moment of special illumination; for others, it takes a long time before we are able to reach a settled mind. God does not deal with us as a crowd, but as individuals. The very process by which he reveals his will to us is part of the special guidance which he has promised to us. His timing, like his wisdom, is absolutely perfect, and we can trust him without reserve.

But, will you?

> *Thy way, not mine, O Lord,*
>   *However dark it be!*
> *Lead me by Thine own hand,*
>   *Choose out the path for me.*
>
> *Smooth let it be or rough,*
>   *It will be still the best;*
> *Winding, or straight, it leads*
>   *Right onward to Thy rest.*
>
> *I dare not choose my lot;*
>   *I would not if I might;*
> *Choose Thou for me, my God,*
>   *So shall I walk aright.*
>
> *The kingdom that I seek*
>   *Is Thine, so let the way*

That leads to it be Thine,
  Else I must surely stray.

Take Thou my cup, and it
  With joy or sorrow fill,
As best to Thee may seem;
  Choose Thou my good and ill.

Choose Thou for me my friends,
  My sickness or my health;
Choose Thou my cares for me,
  My poverty or wealth.

Not mine, not mine the choice,
  In things or great or small;
Be Thou my Guide, my Strength,
  My Wisdom, and my All.

Horatius Bonar

3: *Guarding the Heart*

THE book of Proverbs gives us this counsel:

> Above all else, guard your heart,
> for it is the wellspring of life.
>
> Proverbs 4:23

It is salutary advice. It reminds us that the experience of discovering the will of God has two aspects to it. We have been considering some of the *objective* guidelines which Scripture provides. It lays down a framework of obedience to the revealed will of God. It is there for all of us to see and understand. But there is also a *subjective* element in coming to know God's will. After all, it is my life, not another's, and my obedience, not another's, which are involved in my coming to the conviction that one specific course of action is the Lord's will for my life.

The point of contact between God's revealed will and my personal obedience and walk in his will for my own life lies in the heart. That is why the wise man bids us to guard it – that is, to preserve it in a spirit of sensitive attention to our heavenly Master and King. We are to keep it on alert, as it were, so that he may have his desire in us at a moment's notice.

How are we to maintain this spiritual condition, and

how is it related to the unfolding of the will of God? All the graces which the Spirit works in us, and all the motivations for wholehearted obedience which Scripture presents to us come into focus here. This chapter concentrates on some which have a very special claim for our attention. They are all conditions of the heart which are best learned in youth and developed throughout the whole of life. But there is no stage in life at which they are unimportant. Nor is there a stage in life at which we may comfortably cease from looking to God to help us to grow in these graces.

Motives of the Heart

What makes you want to know the will of God? Why is it so important to you? Among the many motives which God presses upon us in Scripture, there are two which should be singled out for special mention.

1. *The Brevity of Life.* If there is one characteristic which should mark out the believer it is that he or she lives in the consciousness that life has a beginning, a development and an ending. It does not last for ever. The Christian, of all people, seeing his life in the light of eternity, knows that it is short indeed. It is but an interval before eternity dawns, and the curtain is brought down upon the time of our pilgrimage. That is why James says:

> Now listen, you who say, 'Today or tomorrow we will go to this or that city, spend a year there, carry on business and make money.' Why, you do not even know what will happen tomorrow. What is your life? You are a mist that appears for a little while and then vanishes. Instead, you ought to say, 'If it is the Lord's will, we will live and do this or that.'
>
> James 4:13–15

Have you ever grasped that you have only one life to live, and that each day in it can be lived only once? The hours which come fresh to you out of the mercy of your Heavenly Father will carry for ever the imprint which your life leaves on them, until all accounts are closed at his Last Assize. Nothing can ever be returned for minor correction. Life is not only short; it is fleeting. *Now* is the day of salvation, in the fullest possible sense. There is no other 'today' on which we can mark the stamp of obedience to God.

We may naturally be inclined to say that there is still plenty of time to take such serious considerations into account. But we are mistaken, not only because we do not know what a day will bring to us, but because *it does not get easier to have a serious heart in the things of God*. Like produces like in the things of the Spirit. Few Christians who have not early faced up to the brevity of life, and the importance of knowing God's perfect will in its every detail, have been able to develop that spirit at a later stage in life.

Look at Jesus. By the age of *twelve* a spirit of serious concern for his Father's will dominated his life. Already he was enquiring deeply into the significance of God's word for his ministry. By the age of *thirty-three* he was able to say to his Father that he had finished the work for which he had been sent (Jn. 17:4). Now, he is your Example as well as your Saviour!

The Christian who has come to terms with this will not want his life to be given over to petty concerns and interests. Instead his heart will be devoted to the great and vital concerns of living out his brief life in the perfect will of God. Many of us, when it is too late, will realise why the great French pastor Adolphe Monod (1802–56), in his series of short addresses entitled 'A Dying Man's Regrets' listed 'Preoccupation with petty interests' as the last.[1] If there is any sensitivity in our conscience this should reach it.

Have you potentially three score years and ten to live for the Lord Jesus Christ, and yet you have hardly entertained one serious thought about what his will might be? Is it any wonder that guidance seems a problem to us under those circumstances?

If we only began to realise that all flesh is grass, that the wind passes over it and it is gone, would we not make the consecration of our moments and our days a matter of immediate concern? We must guard our hearts precisely here.

2. *The Judgment of God.* We live life under the eye of God, as well as in the light of its brevity. But judgment in the Scriptures must not be confused (as it often is) with condemnation. It may involve that. Clearly the New Testament teaches that, while the Christian is justified by grace he will also be judged by God according to his works (Rom. 2:6–10). He will, however, be judged graciously, as well as justified graciously. The parable of the talents (Matt. 25:14–30) tells of a man who, through the employment of ten talents to the glory of his master, was made ruler over *ten cities*. That is hardly a judgment of merit! It is a reward out of all proportion to what had been accomplished. But that is the nature of God's judgment of our lives. It is suffused with grace, superabounding grace!

All our labours will be judged by God. We shall all appear before the judgment seat of Christ (2 Cor. 5:10). When Paul addressed slaves living at Colosse, he reminded them that their work was meaningful. God's judgment gave it a significance far beyond that

[1] *Adolphe Monod's Farewell* (Banner of Truth edition), 1962, p. 81.

which their earthly masters gave it. This is why the Christian endeavours to do everything to the glory of God; not because of a craven fear of condemnation (although he, too, knows of the terrors of the Lord – 2 Cor. 5:11), but, 'since you know that you will receive an inheritance from the Lord as a reward. It is the Lord Christ you are serving' (Col. 3:22–4). A similar point is made in Ephesians 6:8. God's judgment of the believer's works is according to grace. Which of us, therefore, should not be anxious to please the Lord in all things, knowing that his judgment is our most solemn joy?

All may of Thee partake;
Nothing can be so mean,
Which with this tincture, 'For Thy sake',
Will not grow bright and clean.

A servant with this clause
Makes drudgery divine:
Who sweeps a room, as for Thy laws,
Makes that and the action fine.

George Herbert

Motives, however, never stand alone in Scripture. They are intended to be accompanied by spiritual dispositions, habits and graces of the heart. Again it may be helpful to single out two pairs of these for special mention, because they are closely related to the whole question of God's guidance in our lives.

Conditions in the Heart

One of our greatest failures as Christians is that there can be such a discrepancy between our convictions and the spirit of our lives. We are persuaded, for example, of the grace of God. But our spirit seems to express so little of that same grace. Before God, as we seek his guidance, there must be a developing harmony between our motivations to serve him, and a true condition of the heart. There must be fear and humility, and also obedience and trust.

1. *Fear and Humility.* These graces naturally accompany one another. They promote each other. For fear is a right recognition of God; and such a recognition produces humility before him. That humility will itself bring a certain quality to our fear of the Lord. It will not be craven fear, but the fear of a son, a servant, a subject who loves his Father, his Master and his King. In fact, the two ideas are linked together in a number of places in Scripture, both in our response to God and consequently in our attitude to our fellows (Prov. 15:33; 22:4; 1 Pet. 3:15). The fear of God is particularly crucial, because it lies at the very heart of our relationship to him. It is 'the beginning of wisdom', that is, it is the primary and ruling principle in every wise thought and decision in life.

But what is the fear of God, and how does it come to expression? John Brown describes it well in these words:

We are to fear him: that is, in other words, we are to cherish an awful sense of his infinite grandeur and excellence, corresponding to the revelation he has made of these in his works and word, inducing a conviction that his favour is the greatest of all blessings, and his disapprobation [disapproval] the greatest of all evils, and manifesting itself in leading us practically to seek his favour as the chief good we can enjoy, and avoid his disapprobation as the most tremendous evil we can be subjected to. Such is the fear which the Christian man ought to cherish and manifest towards God.[1]

Charles Bridges expresses it similarly:

But what is this *fear of the Lord*? It is that affectionate reverence, by which the child of God bends himself humbly and carefully to his Father's law.[2]

You will see now why the fear of God is so intimately bound up with his guidance and our obedience. It is the spirit in our hearts which gives glory to God, and produces that fellowship with him which he delights to express in the revelation of his will. It is this same spirit which holds us in the path of his guidance as his will is unfolded before us.

Two passages are specially relevant in understanding this teaching. *Psalm 25* is a development of the theme of the guiding hand of God. It tells us that God 'guides the humble in what is right' (v.9). He instructs the man who fears him in his ways; he confides in those who fear him, and makes known his covenant to them (vv. 12–14). The humble man, in this context, is the man who knows that he has failed, and could so easily fail again. So he asks God to forget the sins of his past life (v. 7), and to show him his ways for the future (v. 4). He displays a spirit of dependence upon God. He knows that he *lacks wisdom*, but he humbly asks God for it, and receives it. When we look at ourselves in the light of this teaching, humility should be one of the fruits of self-examination. We have a duty to be

[1] John Brown, *Expository Discourses on 1 Peter* (Banner of Truth edition), 1975, I, p. 466.
[2] Charles Bridges, *Commentary on Proverbs* (Banner of Truth edition), 1968, pp. 3–4.

sensitive to our own many weaknesses, so that we will always maintain a spirit of childlike dependence on the Lord. We know his greatness and his amazing goodness in forgiving us for the past. So we learn to fear him, lest we offend him again.

Isaiah 11:2–3 takes this theme a little further. It prophesies the character of the coming Messiah. He will delight in the fear of the Lord! Again Charles Bridges has an apt comment:

> *The fear of the Lord* was a lovely grace in the perfect humanity of Jesus (Is. xi. 2, 3). Let it be the test of our 'predestination to be conformed to his image' (Rom. 8:29). It is the genuine spirit of adoption. The child of God has only one dread – to offend his Father; only one desire – to please and delight in him . . . 'The heart that is touched with the loadstone of Divine love, trembles still with godly fear' (Leighton on 1 Pet. 2:17).[1]

There is a most interesting connection in Isaiah's words between the fear of God and the knowledge of his will and ways:

> The Spirit of the Lord will rest on him –
>   the Spirit of wisdom and of understanding,
>   the Spirit of counsel and of power,
>   the Spirit of knowledge and of the fear of the
>   Lord –
> and he will delight in the fear of the Lord.
>
> He will not judge by what he sees with his eyes,
>   or decide by what he hears with his ears . . .
>
> Isaiah 11:2–3

---

[1] *Ibid*, p. 87.

In fact, the fear of the Lord and the knowledge of his will were almost synonymous in the life of his Servant Jesus (cf. Prov. 2:6; 9:10). He has set us a most beautiful example of the spirit which should accompany the seeking and doing of the will of God.

Perhaps this is why, in the New Testament, fear and humility became characteristics of the obedience of the church and its discovery of God's constant guidance (cf. Acts 2:43; 5:5; 5:11; 9:31). When we fear the Lord we depart from evil and do good (2 Cor. 7:1). We live our lives as strangers here in reverent fear (1 Pet. 1:17).

Do you know something of this?

> *There is no joy the soul can meet*
> *   Upon life's various road*
> *Like the sweet fear that sits and shrinks*
> *   Under the eye of God*
>
> *A special joy is in all love*
> *   For objects we revere;*
> *Thus joy in God will always be*
> *   Proportioned to our fear.*
>
> *Oh Thou art greatly to be feared,*
> *   Thou art so prompt to bless!*
> *The dread to miss such love as Thine*
> *   Makes fear but love's excess.*
>
> *But fear is love, and love is fear*
> *   And in and out they move;*
> *But fear is an intenser joy*
> *   Than mere unfrightened love.*

When most I fear Thee, Lord! then most
  Familiar I appear;
And I am in my soul most free,
  When I am most in fear.

I feel Thee most a Father, when
  I fancy Thee most near:
And Thou comest not so nigh in love
  As Thou comest, Lord! in fear.

They love Thee little, if at all,
  Who do not fear Thee much;
If love is Thine attraction, Lord!
  Fear is Thy very touch.

F. W. Faber

2. *Obedience and Trust.* You will be accustomed to reading, or singing these words in the reverse order:

Trust and obey,
For there's no other way
To be happy in Jesus,
But to trust and obey.

But this is not a matter of trusting and then obeying. It is also a matter of obeying and continuing to trust in God, even when we cannot understand his ways with us. Abraham trusted where he could not see (Heb. 11:8). But even when trust wavered, obedience was the only way into the perfect will of God for his life (Rom. 4:18; Heb. 11:17–19).

We find this combination of graces again in Psalm 25. The ways of the Lord are guaranteed to be loving and faithful for those who keep the demands of God's covenant (however opaque they may be to the eye of the flesh). This is the kind of obedience which sustains us in the will of God. Indeed, so much is this the case, that Proverbs hints that a natural relationship develops between the obedient heart and a tendency to walk in the will of God:

The integrity of the upright guides them,
　but the unfaithful are destroyed by their
　duplicity.

The righteousness of the upright delivers them,
　but the unfaithful are trapped by evil desires.

Righteousness guards the man of integrity,
　but wickedness overthrows the sinner.

Proverbs 11:3, 6; 13:6

Here is an immensely important lesson to learn as early as we can in the Christian life. Be obedient even when you do not know where obedience may lead you. It will guard you and protect you. Always trust God's word and live by his commands rather than by circumstances, providences or opportunities alone. Only in obedience, in a trust which clings to the promise that God is working everything together for those who love him, can there ever be safety. For only in obedience can we discover the great joy of the will of God.

The condition of the heart determines the quality of our life in the natural realm. A diseased heart has a debilitating influence on every aspect of our experience. The same is true in the Christian life. That is why we must exercise the heart in godly thinking, trusting obedience, humility and the fear of God.

When our hearts grow strong in these graces, we will find what pleasure God has in revealing to us the outworking of his covenant promises in our individual lives.

4: *A Christian Life-style*

So far we have seen that the chief means of discovering the special, personal will of God for our lives is by obedience to his revealed will in Scripture. In a sense, knowing the Lord's will involves us in a continuing series of decisions and choices. We must choose the way of the Lord, rather than the way of our own or the world's devising.

In every age of God's kingdom his people have been very conscious of this. The Book of Psalms opens with words which set the key of the whole Psalter. It reminds us that two ways lie before all men. There is the way of the righteous, and there is the way of the wicked. The Lord 'watches over the way of the righteous' (Ps. 1:6). In other words, he guides them in the path of his blessings as they walk on the road of obedience.

This emphasis on 'the two ways' (as it came to be known) is a marked feature of Christian teaching. One of the earliest documents of the Christian church, called *The Didache*, illustrates this. It begins: 'There are two ways, one of life and one of death; and between the two ways there is a great difference'. Its opening chapters expound the theme in detail. But this is no more than a continuation of the emphasis of the New Testament. Many of the parables of Jesus hint at the same thing as they face us with two alternatives in life. More explicitly we find this theme running through

Paul's letters. There is the way of the flesh *or* the way of the Spirit. There is the way of sight *or* there is the way of faith. We are to choose one rather than the other. We are to pursue one and flee from the other. In doing so we walk in the way of the Lord.

The letter to the Ephesians comprehensively emphasises this teaching. There (as in Col. 1:10; 1 Thess. 2:12) Paul speaks about *walking worthily*, adopting a life-style which is truly in the will of God. In the rest of this chapter we shall examine the teaching he gives.

Ephesians is perhaps the most magnificent of all Paul's letters. It is usually regarded today as a circular letter (hence the total lack of personal greetings and also the general nature of its contents). The copy of the letter which we possess was the one which was sent to Ephesus. Paul's theme is God's wonderful grace. He expounds its amazing dimensions in the opening verses of the letter. God's grace toward us began in eternity. He chose us in Christ before the foundation of the world (Eph. 1:4). His love touches us in time, through the work of Christ and the Spirit (Eph. 1:12–13). God's grace will bring us to his eternal glory when we shall enjoy all the blessings of being his adopted sons and daughters (Eph. 1:5, 10, 14). It turns dead, rebellious sinners into resurrected, obedient children (2:1–10).

The message of grace does not stop there. It is fascinating to watch the development of Paul's thinking in these chapters. From the beginning of chapter 3 it is obvious that he is straining to *apply* the grace of God to the issues of practical Christian living. 'Because of this grace' he says 'I, Paul, the prisoner of Christ Jesus for you Gentiles . . .' – and it is undoubtedly his intention to say: 'I beg you to live a life, to walk in a way which is utterly consistent with what God's grace has done for you'. But Paul cannot write the word 'Gentiles' without being caught up in sheer amazement that *now*, during his lifetime, and largely through his own ministry, the gospel has broken out of its Jewish confines. God's grace is reaching all nations! So, in a sense he goes off at a tangent from the point he intended to make.

Exactly the same thing happens at the beginning of Ephesians 4! Similar words are used: 'I urge you to walk worthy of your calling'. But as he begins to expand his theme, he finds that it is necessary to explain the great doctrine of the unity, diversity and resulting harmony of grace in the church. Eventually, in chapter 4:17 he returns to the theme which he had begun in chapter 3.

Sometimes in modern translations this connection is obscured. But in older translations (A.V., R.V.) the word 'walk' is used constantly (2:2; 2:10; 4:1; 4:17; 5:2; 5:8; 5:15). If you mark your Bible, mark these verses, and you will notice how clearly the theme of *the Christian walk* is being developed in this letter. The Christian is a new man, and he must therefore walk like a new man (Eph. 4:17–24). Just as a man, dominated and controlled by alcohol will evidence this in his *walk*, so the man who is under the control of the Spirit will demonstrate it by the way he walks in the will of God (Eph. 5:18). He will let the word of Christ dwell in him richly (Col. 3:16). In other words, he will discover the Lord's will for his life by obedience to the Lord's will for the life of every believer. This will is made known to us in Scripture.

How are we to walk worthy of God? Paul indicates that it is by living in a way that is consistent with his revealed character. In the earlier part of the letter he had spoken about (1) the revelation of God's love (1:4);

(2) the illumination of God's people by his grace (1:17);
(3) the revelation of God's wisdom in salvation (3:10).
Now, in chapter 5, he takes up these themes and
demonstrates how the Christian life is consistent with
them. *To live in the will of God is to walk in love, to walk
in light and to walk in wisdom.*

Walking in Love

Be ye therefore imitators of God, as beloved children; and
walk in love, even as Christ also loved you, and gave
himself up for us, an offering and a sacrifice to God for an
odour of a sweet smell.

But fornication, and all uncleanness, or covetousness,
let it not even be named among you, as becometh saints:
nor filthiness, nor foolish talking, or jesting, which are
not befitting: but rather giving of thanks.

For this ye know of a surety, that no fornicator, nor
unclean person, nor covetous man, who is an idolater,
hath any inheritance in the kingdom of Christ and God.
Let no man deceive you with empty words: for because of
these things cometh the wrath of God upon the sons of
disobedience.

Ephesians 5:1–6 (A.S.V.)

What does it mean to 'walk in love'? Paul expresses
it both positively and negatively. *Positively* it means to
follow the example of Christ's love, demonstrated on
the cross. True walking in love means giving oneself to
and for others. That is an unalterable principle of
living in the will of God. Martin Luther used to say
that the trouble with man is that he is *incurvatus in se*
– turned in upon himself. He has distorted the purposes
of God for his life by living for himself. But grace
changes this, and works to change it more and more,
in order to produce Christlikeness in us. Walking in

the will of God means living as an offering to God and as a living sacrifice for others (Rom. 12:1–2).

Paul also expresses walking in love *negatively*. That is arresting in our modern climate of opinion where it is so superficially assumed that the one thing which love never does is to say 'No'. This is a radically mistaken view. You will notice that in these opening verses in Ephesians 5, Paul provides a substantial (but still not exhaustive) list of all the practices to which love will say 'No'. Walking in the ways of God means *refusing* other ways!

Why should this be? It is because *love is the fulfilling of the law*. Love therefore turns from breaking the law. Love knows that there are many activities over which it will write 'No-No' (Rom. 13:8–10).

Have you ever noticed how clearly this negative emphasis appears in Paul's description of love in 1 Corinthians 13?

> Love does *not* envy
> Love does *not* boast
> Love is *not* proud
> Love is *not* rude
> Love is *not* self-seeking
> Love is *not* easily-angered
> Love does *not* keep records of wrongs
> Love does *not* delight in evil

It is for this reason that Paul describes covetousness as idolatry in Ephesians 5:5. We do not usually associate these two things together quite so closely. But in the New Testament's way of thinking, the opposite of love for God is love for self. And love for self is a form of idolatry, just as it is the root of covetousness.

Guidance, knowing and doing God's will, as we are

now beginning to see, is a moral, not merely an intellectual issue. Just so, love is also a moral issue. It is not merely a matter of feelings. It involves decisions of the heart. To be walking in the will of God implies that some measure of this quality of Christian love is being exhibited in our lives. At the very least, if we say we desire the will of God we must make love our aim (1 Cor. 14:1).

Walking in the Light

There is a recurring theme in this teaching which Paul had already intimated at the beginning of the chapter. His call is that we should imitate God as his beloved children.

These words are important. For one thing they show us that God does not throw us back on our own resources or devices in the Christian life. He makes us his children – his much-loved children – and he gives us the Spirit of adoption (Rom. 8:15; Gal. 4:5–6). For the Christian child of his heavenly Father, like the ordinary child of an earthly father, imitation, mimicry, is a natural consequence of his sonship! So, Paul urges us: Mimic God, imitate him! Be like him! He has shown you his love; therefore, love. He has also brought you out of darkness into his light; therefore, walk in the light.

What are the features of this walking in the light?

Be not ye therefore partakers with them: for ye were once darkness, but are now light in the Lord: walk as children of light (for the fruit of the light is in all goodness and righteousness and truth), proving what is well-pleasing unto the Lord: and have no fellowship with the unfruitful works of darkness, but rather even reprove them: for the things which are done by them in secret it is a shame even to speak of. But all things when they are reproved are made manifest by the light: for everything that is made manifest is light. Wherefore he saith, Awake, thou that sleepest, and arise from the dead, and Christ shall shine upon thee.

Ephesians 5:7–14 (A.S.V.)

The first characteristic of walking in the light is *separation*. The child of God will not become a partner in sin, nor with men in the pursuit of sin. Paul does not mean that the Christian is to become *isolated from* his fellows (See 1 Cor. 5:9–10). Rather, he is to be *distinguished from* them by the life-style which he adopts. This is a possibility for him because of the second characteristic – his life is identified by *contrast*. He was once darkness, but now he is light in the Lord! He once walked as a spiritually dead man, following the course of this world and the prince of the power of the air, chasing his own passions (Eph. 2:1–4). *But no longer*. Now he has entered God's marvellous light. He is changed. The transformation can be seen. What has happened to him can only be described in terms of the contrast of light breaking into the darkness at creation, for 'God, who said, "Let light shine out of darkness," made his light shine in our hearts to give us the light of the knowledge of the glory of God in the face of Christ' (2 Cor. 4:5). This was what happened dramatically to Paul on the Damascus Road. But it happens to every believer. He is brought into the light. He is different from what he once was apart from the grace of God. He is different from what he would have become apart from the grace of God.

The direct consequence of this is that the Christian's life-style will 'reprove', 'convict' or expose the life-style of the world (Eph. 5:13). The same verb is used in John 16:8–11 of the ministry of the Holy

Spirit. He works powerfully in the hearts of men in order to convict them of the true nature of their sin against Christ. His light makes them conscious of the darkness which has gripped their minds (cf. Eph. 4:17–19). Paul does not mean that the Christian's obedience to the will of God requires that he should always go around pointing an accusing finger at others. That is the high road to Pharisaism. He is speaking about a work which is done in others' lives of which we ourselves may not be conscious – the saltiness of Christian holiness rubbing into the wounds of a conscience awakened to personal sin and guilt.

Paul's teaching is far-reaching in its implications. For it suggests that obedience to the will of God involves us in a life which is a stark contrast to the life of the world. There is no sincerity in our profession to want the will of God in our lives if we are not in tune with his will for personal holiness. Paul puts his finger on several sensitive areas in these verses. If we would walk in the light, we must live distinctively, in a way that contrasts obviously with ungodliness:

> *Set up Thy standard, Lord, that we*
> *Who claim a heavenly birth,*
> *May march with Thee to smite the lies*
> *That vex Thy groaning earth.*

> *Yet who can fight for truth and God,*
> *Enthralled by lies and sin?*
> *He who would wage such war on earth*
> *Must first be true within.*

O God of truth for whom we long,
O Thou that hearest prayer,
Do Thine own battle in our hearts,
And slay the falsehood there.

Thomas Hughes

Wake up, O sleeper,
  rise from the dead,
And Christ will shine on you!

Ephesians 5:14

Walking in Wisdom

Look therefore carefully how ye walk, not as unwise, but as wise; redeeming the time, because the days are evil. Wherefore be ye not foolish, but understand what the will of the Lord is. And be not drunken with wine, wherein is riot, but be filled with the Spirit.

Ephesians 5:15–18 (A.S.V.)

We are to walk, not as unwise, foolish Christians. (Paul does not deny that Christians could be *both*; he emphasises that they ought not to be *either*). Wisdom and the will of God are intimately related, as the Book of Proverbs underlines. Nothing is more vital for practical knowledge of the purposes of God than wisdom:

Get wisdom, get understanding;
do not forget my words or swerve from them.
Do not forsake wisdom, and she will protect you;
love her, and she will watch over you.
Wisdom is supreme; therefore get wisdom.
Though it cost all you have, get understanding.

Esteem her, and she will exalt you;
　embrace her and she will honour you.
She will set a garland of grace on your head
and present you with a crown of splendour.

Proverbs 4:5-9

But what does walking in wisdom imply? Again Paul has spelled it out for us to follow.

To walk in wisdom means to walk *carefully*. The word is *akribōs*, which is used in Matthew 2:8 and Luke 1:3 in ways which help us to appreciate its significance here. When Herod heard of the birth of another king, he exhorted the wise men to 'Go and make a careful search for the child'. When Luke wrote his Gospel he 'carefully investigated everything from the beginning'. *Akribōs* means accurately, carefully, down to the last detail.

Does Paul mean that the Christian becomes a pernickety character always fussing about little details, and arguing about the importance of trivialities? No! He does not mean that our faithfulness to Christ makes secondary things take primary place in our thinking. Rather he means that faithfulness to Christ extends to every detail of our lives. No part of them will remain untouched by the influence of wisdom. We will take loving care to be obedient to the Lord.

In fact, Paul himself tells us what he means by walking carefully. He says that it involves 'redeeming the time'. He uses the word *kairos* which means 'opportunity'. The wise man sees that opportunities need to be 'redeemed'. They may have to be purchased at the expense of something else. That does not mean that the Christian will become preoccupied with petty concerns. The very reverse should be true. He will be careful to set his sight on those issues in life which are of great spiritual moment.

You say that you want to find the will of God in your life. But are you walking wisely, in the sense of walking carefully? Are you attending to your opportunities? Few things are more common among those who complain that guidance has become a very frustrating thing for them than the failure to use the present opportunities God has given to them! Be careful, then, how you walk. Walk wisely!

To walk in wisdom also means to walk *intelligently*. We are summoned to 'understand what the Lord's will is' (Eph. 5:17). The Christian's obedience to the leading of God is an understanding, intelligent pursuit of what God has revealed. It is never a mindless exercise (cf. 1 Cor. 14:20). We are to 'find out what pleases the Lord' (Eph. 5:10).

If we read these statements with a little care, we shall at once be delivered from the mistaken idea that guidance is something which comes like a bolt from the blue and overtakes us. It is not. Guidance is the way in which God leads us as we think through the implications of his truth, and seek to find practical application of it in our lives. It involves using our minds to think through the path which God wants us to take in his service. It requires familiarity with Scripture, and fellowship with the Spirit, who alone knows the mind of God (1 Cor. 2:11–13).

To walk in wisdom consequently means to walk *spiritually*, under the controlling grace of the Holy Spirit. This is why Paul urges us *in this context* to be filled with the Spirit. The parallel passage in Colossians 3:16 replaces this exhortation with 'Let the word of Christ dwell in you richly'. It suggests that there is an intimate relationship between exposing ourselves to the rule of the Spirit and exposing ourselves to obedience to the word of God. Wherever we search in Scripture for teaching on the guidance of God, we invariably meet this combination. Guidance is supernatural; the will of God is made known to us spiritually. That is why we need to walk in the Spirit. But it is also made known to us through the word. That is why we must walk *intelligently* in the Spirit.

The hall-mark of the Christian's walk in this segment of Paul's teaching is thankfulness. We are to be 'always giving thanks to God the Father for everything, in the name of our Lord Jesus Christ' (Eph. 5:20). Thanksgiving takes the place of sin (Eph. 5:4). Always! For everything!

Why should this be so? It is because those who walk in love, in the light, and in wisdom, develop an assurance that, whatever their failures, they are walking on the path in which all of God's promises may be received. They know that, however dark and dangerous this path may be, they could not be happier or safer anywhere else. In the knowledge that they are living in obedience to God, all the circumstances and providences of life can be accepted gladly as from the hand of their Father in heaven. To him they can go with the fears and anxieties which his will seems to have cast on their lives. They know that he is using all of these experiences to transform them into the image of Christ. For this he has predestined them. They know of a certainty therefore that all things will co-operate for their good, and that nothing can ever separate them from the love of God in the Lord Jesus Christ! *That is why they are able to be thankful to the Lord for the ways in which he has brought them.*

The Christian who walks in love, in the light and in wisdom will be a thankful Christian. That will make him distinctive. He knows in measure *now* what he will know in full measure *hereafter*:

> *With mercy and with judgment*
> *My web of time He wove,*
> *And aye the dews of sorrow*
> *Were lustred with his love:*
> *I'll bless the hand that guided,*
> *I'll bless the heart that planned,*
> *When throned where glory dwelleth*
> *In Immanuel's land.*

Anne Ross Cousin

5: *Principles of Conduct*

 UR previous chapter emphasised the fact that walking in the will of God produces a distinctive life-style. There will be certain characteristics which will be true of all Christians in all places and in every age. There are abiding qualities about true Christians which would make them recognisable by their fellow believers in very different epochs of church history.

But for every Christian the question arises, not, What is true of all Christians always? but, *What is the will of God in this particular, unique situation in which I find myself?* We have to face the issue of the nature of the principles which govern Christian conduct. How do we discover the will of God when we are faced with a possibly bewildering array of choices?

In chapter four, we noticed that the exposition of the Christian walk was a major theme in one of Paul's letters. This further question of the governing principles which lead us into the will of God for our lives is also a theme with which Paul dealt at some length. We find him discussing it in his First Letter to the Corinthians.

The Corinthians were in danger of doing what we have underlined should never be done. They had begun to divorce the spiritual from the ethical. They were largely taken up with spiritual gifts and experiences, and they had ignored the fact that the gospel has a cutting ethical edge to it. The Spirit who is given to us to lavish his gifts upon us is a *Holy* Spirit. Unless his love is produced in us all our gifts will profit us nothing. This is the message. Instead of heeding it, the Corinthians were so mesmerised by their new-found liberty of spirit that they had introduced a new catch-phrase into the current jargon of their little fellowship: 'everything is permissible' (1 Cor. 6:12; 10:23).

We can easily translate this into the kind of catch-phrase which might arise among Christians today. Indeed one does not need to *invent* the parallels. They already exist: 'You can take Jesus anywhere'. It is not so very long ago that Augustine's old dictum was on the lips of many people: 'Love God and do what you like'. The problem, of course, is that even short and snappy phrases like these are further abbreviated. They become 'anywhere' and 'do what you like'. That was what had happened in Corinth. There had been a severing of spiritual liberty from moral responsibility.

Paul took up this question in two sections of his letter – 1 Corinthians 6:9–20 and 10:23–11:1. The details of the situations he was discussing need not concern us here. They do not make pleasant reading. What is of interest to us is that it was in this context that Paul gave the Corinthians certain principles by which to regulate their conduct. He explained how they could discover what was really consistent with the will of God for their lives in every situation. He wanted to show them how to relate the freedom of the children of God with their responsibilities to live lives fully pleasing to him and obedient to his will.

Paul's principles remain valid. Not only so; they are of great practical usefulness to us in discerning what the will of the Lord is in our lives. A careful study of them gives rise to a series of questions which will help to unfold what God's guidance might be in any given situation.

1. *Is it Lawful?*

The Corinthians emphasised the (biblical) principle that Christ had set them free. Paul retorted that *freedom is not the only principle in the Christian life*. Freedom is *for* something. God has set us free for holiness. He has set us free from the guilt and bondage of sin – but not in order that we might become enslaved to the very sins for which Christ died to redeem us!

This is powerfully reinforced by the apostle (in 1 Cor. 6:9–11). Paul provides a long list of the kinds of sinful conduct which are contrary to membership of the kingdom of God. He does not mean that these heinous sins are the unforgivable sin. Some of the Corinthians had indulged in these very sins before they were converted. Yet they had been washed, sanctified and justified through Christ! But they had to be radically converted in order to be fitted for the kingdom of God. No anarchy is present there – it is a kingdom, a monarchy, and is governed by the great and holy commandments of God.

What is Paul's point? It is that *no action which is contrary to the plain word of God can ever be legitimate for the Christian.* No appeal to spiritual freedom or to providential circumstances can ever make what is ethically wrong anything else but sinful. For the Christian is free only to love and obey the law of God. Therein lies his true freedom.

We can often reduce the possible choices that face us at different times in our lives by this very simple question: *Is it lawful?* How readily Satan seems to be able to blind us just here – and we lose sight of the fact that we have been saved in order to be made holy.

2. *Is it Beneficial to Me?*

If our first question is concerned with the nature of the action itself, our second one must be concerned with its consequences. It may be true (in a sense) says Paul, that 'all things are permissible' (cf. I Tim. 4:4; Rom. 14:14 etc.). 'But not everything is beneficial' (I Cor. 6:12).

Do you ever find yourself challenged on a course of action by a fellow-Christian, and automatically respond: 'What's wrong with it?'. It is the most natural form of self-defence. But it may well hide a guilty conscience. For, in our heart of hearts we know, as Paul so incisively teaches, that this is not the really important question. There may be 'nothing wrong with it'; but there may be nothing right with it; it may not prove to be beneficial to me.

The question I must learn to ask is: Will it bring benefits, as far as I am able to judge, so that my relationship to the Lord Jesus Christ is strengthened? Will it draw me nearer to him?

There are so many areas in which this applies. When I am faced with a choice of occupation, or a sphere of work, or a move to another part of the country, with all that it involves in terms of fellowship, ministry and spiritual influence, I am surely obliged to ask this question. Of course it is not the all-determining factor in each instance. But it is an important factor in many cases.

I may find myself with the opportunity to spend a sum of money on something on which I have set my heart. But is it God's will? Well, let the question be introduced into my thinking: Will it benefit? Or, will it have the tendency to consume my time, energy and interests in such a way that I will be spiritually the poorer? Will it complicate, rather than simplify my life?

Of course no two people will give exactly the same answer in every situation. We are no longer speaking about whether a course of action is lawful for the Christian. We are considering only actions which are. But something which has a neutral influence on one person may be detrimental to another. We are not called to judge other men's consciences (1 Cor. 2:15; 4:3–5). But 'the spiritual man makes judgments about all things', and this is what we are enabled to do when we ask: 'Is it beneficial to me?'. It may or may not be in others' experience. That is not my concern. I am responsible to Christ for my own stewardship. Is this beneficial to *me*?

3. *Is it Enslaving?*

'Everything is permissible to me' – but I will not be mastered by anything (1 Cor. 6:12). There is a play on words in what Paul says: These things are all within my power – but will I end up in their power? Again, assuming that what is being considered falls into the category of things legitimate, this question can only ultimately be answered in personal terms.

What is the principle? It is that the Christian must always, through the grace of the Spirit, be master of himself. Paul illustrates this later in 1 Corinthians. In the race all who compete have already gone into strict training. They have sought to master and subdue all their natural appetites so that, instead of being mastered by them, they will master their bodies and make them their slaves (1 Cor. 9:27).

What happens to the athlete who nibbles at cream cakes and tucks away too many calories? A moment comes in the race when he ceases to be the master, and the appetites to which he has yielded strangle every last ounce of energy out of him. They have him at their mercy and all hopes of winning the prize must be abandoned.

Is there not a clear parallel in the Christian life? It is possible to make choices which, eventually, will tend to squeeze out our spiritual energies; to commit ourselves to things which, however legitimate in general terms, will eventually become the dominating and driving force in our lives.

Of course we have our spiritual liberties. But when we find ourselves unable to enjoy the Christian life without our liberties, then we have become enslaved to them. There is, for example, presumably no built-in evil about owning a new car, or living in a pleasant house, or enjoying various foods, spending time in various pursuits, or with certain kinds of people. But when we cannot be content without them; when we simply *must* have them – they are no longer our liberties, but our chains. The Christian should develop in Christ a sensitivity to those things to which he will most readily allow himself to be brought into bondage. 'Will this enslave me?' will be a question never far from his thinking. 'I will not be mastered by anything' is a good motto text for the man who has received a spirit of self-discipline (2 Tim. 1:7).

4. *Is it Consistent with Christ's Lordship?*

Sin of tragic proportions had erupted in the congregation at Corinth. Consequently Paul asks whether they rightly understood their relationship to *the Lord*. The only chapter in which he does not use this title for Jesus is chapter 13! It deeply troubled him that the Corinthians failed to realise that they were not their own; they had been bought at the great price of their Master's life blood (1 Cor. 6:19–20; 7:23).

What is Paul's concern? It is that whenever a Christian engages in a course of action he does so in union with Christ. *Nothing* severs that relationship. Not even sin can annul it. That is the horrific truth. Whenever the Corinthians gave themselves to gross and indecent sin, *they were dragging Christ into it*.

Sometimes we say that the principle by which any action may be judged is: Can I take Christ there? There is truth in that. But it is not the whole truth. For, Paul emphasises, we have no choice in the matter. We *do* take Christ there. As those who are united to him we cannot leave him behind. So the real question is: Can I take Christ there and look him in the face without shame? Is this course of action, this decision I am taking, totally consistent with my personal confession that 'Jesus Christ is my Lord'?

Again it should be emphasised that on its own this question is of limited help. It may answer my questions about the Lord's will immediately (particularly if the answer is 'No'). But it is not in itself an all-sufficient test. It is not the final litmus paper by which we can judge the Lord's will. We need to take all these questions into consideration. We may find, having sought to answer them all, that there is still a momentous decision which God expects us to make. But it can hardly be doubted that much confused thinking began to be cleared away from the church at Corinth as these penetrating questions were set before them. We too will find the same.

5. *Is it Helpful to Others?*

When we move further on in the first letter to Corinth, we find Paul asks similar questions of a different situation – an indication that we are on the right track when we assume that these questions have a wide and valuable application to many areas of our thinking. But he added others.

I must not rest content with asking whether a course of action will be personally helpful. Will it have a like beneficial effect on others? Indeed, do I engage in it with a view to serving and helping them? Or, am I in danger of 'destroying the work of God' (Rom. 14:20)? When speaking of the Christian's personal freedom, and the way it must be balanced over against the weaknesses and strengths of others, Paul confesses: 'I try to please everyone in every way. For I am not seeking my own good, but the good of many, so that they may be saved. Follow my example . . .' (1 Cor. 10:33).

Jesus lived by this principle. When he summarised his commitment in his great prayer to the Father, he said: 'I am sanctifying myself *for their sakes*' (Jn. 17:19). We should be concerned to help and please others, Paul affirms, 'For even Christ did not please himself (Rom. 15:3). Does this not drive home to us the fact that the will of God (and therefore his guidance) is the most demanding thing in the world? Does it not pierce to the dividing place in our lives between soul and spirit (Heb. 4:12)? For we are often concerned with guidance in order that our lives may be freed from anxiety and uncertainty – so that we may have a measure of personal comfort and security. God, on the other hand, is concerned that we should be cast upon him to do his will, *whatever the enduring cost*. The will of God is shaped in the image of his Son's cross. The will of God means death to our own will, and resurrection only when we have died to all our own plans.

Did we really appreciate that this was what we were letting ourselves in for when we said that we wanted guidance?

6. *Is it Consistent with Biblical Example?*

Do not be surprised that Paul's discussion reaches its conclusion with these words: 'Follow my example, as I follow the example of Christ' (1 Cor. 11:1).

'What would Paul have done?' 'What would Christ himself have done?'. These are the questions we can now ask. Are there incidents, or is there teaching in Scripture, which can be applied to the situation in which I find myself? Will it give me a clue to the will of God for my life now? (Cf Phil. 3:17; 2 Thess. 3:7; 2 Tim. 3:10; Heb. 6:12; 13:7.)

We are not left to our own imagination in dealing with this question. The only Christ we know – for that matter the only Paul we know – is to be found in the pages of Scripture. Here again we are driven back to our great principle: we discover the will of God by a sensitive application of Scripture to our own lives.

The apostle Peter speaks in similar vein. Christ suffered for us, and in doing so he left us *an example* that we should follow in his footsteps (1 Pet. 2:21). He uses a very picturesque word, which means a model or pattern to be copied. It is the kind of expression we would use of a teacher's light pencil outline which a child would fill in with a heavier hand, and fill out in his own unique way. What a picture of the Christian life! Christ teaches us to live by faith by walking his life before us, and then saying: 'Now, put your feet into these footprints of mine, and you will soon learn'.

This is exactly what we are to do. We are to go over

the lines which Christ has drawn in, lines which we find in the Scriptures. We are to take his hand, and find his footprints in Scripture, and then to follow them. Because of his apostolic ministry Paul was able to encourage his contemporaries to follow him because he followed Christ. There is still an application of that which will benefit us in our thinking.

Yet, even here, Paul cannot escape from the ultimate challenge, 'whatever you do, do it all for the glory of God' (1 Cor. 10:31). We cannot escape this challenge either. It is the non-negotiable norm of Christian living. If my heart goes out for his glory, then I will find the yoke of these questions is easy, and the burden of gospel holiness to which they urge me is light indeed:

Is it lawful?
Is it beneficial?
Is it enslaving?
Is it consistent with the Lordship of Christ?
Is it beneficial to others?
Is it consistent with the example of Christ and the apostles?

Is it for the glory of God? For that matter, am I living for the glory of God?

> *The task Thy wisdom hath assigned*
> *O let me cheerfully fulfil,*
> *In all my works Thy presence find,*
> *And prove Thy good and perfect will.*
>
> *Thee may I set at my right hand,*
> *Whose eyes my inmost substance see,*
> *And labour on at Thy command,*
> *And offer all my works to Thee.*

> *Give me to bear Thy easy yoke,*
> *And every moment watch and pray,*
> *And still to things eternal look,*
> *And hasten to Thy glorious day.*

Charles Wesley

6: *Consider Your Calling*

W̶E spend more time pursuing our life-calling than anything else we do. Less time is spent in leisure, in study, in the activities of family life, than is spent at the work to which God calls us.

For the Christian the choice of a life-calling will be seen as one of the most important decisions he ever makes. It will determine many aspects of his life. It is essential therefore to be assured that we are doing the will of God.

But, what does God want me to do? How shall I recognise his calling? Has he something specific for me to do?

We must first set this question against the general background of biblical teaching. Have you ever noticed, in studying the Ten Commandments, that the one we usually associate with keeping a sabbath day is really a commandment about the way we keep God's commandments every day? We are to sanctify six days of the week by completing our work during them. We are to sanctify the seventh by resting from labour and worshipping the Lord: 'Six days you shall labour and do all your work, but the seventh day is a Sabbath to the Lord your God. On it you shall not do any work . . .' (Ex. 20:9–10).

Work is a privilege. It is the gift of God. But it is also a commandment and a duty. God has given it to us to make us complete men and women. Indeed, Scripture indicates that when we work we reflect the image of God, just as when we take a sabbath rest we pattern our behaviour on our Maker: 'For in six days the Lord made the heavens and the earth, the sea, and all that is in them, but he rested on the seventh day. Therefore the Lord blessed the Sabbath day and made it holy' (Ex. 20:11).

Jesus worked. For most of his life he was a carpenter – probably a craftsman. Wood was his medium. He was, as we might say, 'good with his hands'.

It is a great tragedy that we have lost sight of what Jesus did. I went to a school where only those who failed to make the grade in the more academic subjects ever took wood-work, or crafts classes. Some of us worked with our 'brains', others with our 'hands'. Or so it was thought. But most of us, indeed all of us, really needed to work with both. There might be less industrial relations problems today if there had been fewer schools like mine yesterday!

Jesus worked with his hands, and he also worked with his mind. He did not think manual labour was less important to God than mental activity. He did not think that white-collar work was better than blue-collar work. He knew that both were God's gifts, and so he enjoyed both. He was able to keep the great minds of the church of his time ticking over with profound questions when he was twelve (Lk. 2:46–7). But he also found deep satisfaction when he was carving and working at the carpenter's bench.

Jesus knew the early chapters of Genesis. He discovered there that when God made man he gave him much to think about: How was he going to rule over this wonderful world in which he had been placed? What would he call these animals God had given him? (See Gen. 1:26; 2:19ff.) But man also had work to do with

his hands. He had to look after the garden (Gen. 2:15).
He did not yet find frustration and toil in that work
(Gen. 3:17–19); but it was work, hard work none the
less. He was blessed through it; he found great pleasure
in it. At the end of the day he should have been able to
look up at the stars, and sing to God before he went to
sleep:

When I consider your heavens,
   the work of your fingers,
the moon and the stars,
   which you have set in place,
what is man that you are mindful of him,
   the son of man that you care for him?
You made him a little lower than the heavenly
   beings
   and crowned him with glory and honour.

You made him ruler over the works of your hands;
   you put everything under his feet:
all flocks and herds,
   and the beasts of the field,
the birds of the air,
   and the fish of the sea,
   all that swim the paths of the seas.

O Lord, our Lord,
   how majestic is your name in all the earth!

Psalm 8:3–9

When the Christian serves God in his daily work, he
too may lie down at night with the same spirit of
thanksgiving and joy. He knows that his daily work is
not an unfortunate addition to the Christian life. It is

part and parcel of it. Along with home and family life, the fellowship of God's people and his service, our life calling is promised blessing by the Lord.

But do we bring right motivations to it? Do we want to give our best to our work because we see the privilege of it? Do we want to consecrate ourselves to the Lord's will because we know that the eye of the Master is upon us? Do we really believe that work is a privilege and dignity which God has graciously bestowed on his children?

If we do, it is important to have a clear grasp of the –

Considerations Which Help us to Identify our Calling

At the end of the day, *we* will have to decide what the will of God is! We get very readily confused here about false ideas of the nature of God's guidance. We look for supernatural revelations, when God means us to live by his word. We want to abandon our normal thought-processes, when God wants us to bear the burden of thinking through his purposes for our lives. We want to know immediately and intuitively what we are to do, when he wants to prepare us for the task by the slow, and sometimes painful process of waiting.

Time and time again people who have read the 'standard' books and booklets on guidance complain that they did not really find them helpful. What they often mean is that they did not discover their personal calling by reading a booklet on guidance! As if God would deposit his personal, eternally purposed will for the life of every Christian in a booklet! No, his will cannot be known apart from the process of discovering it as time unfolds.

The biographies of God's people in Scripture should

make this principle clear to us. Take Abraham. Did he not go out *not knowing where he was going*, not really sure of what God had planned? (See Heb. 11:8.) But he acted on the clear revelation of the will of God. Or, take Joseph. God had given him some intimation of his destiny in the dream he foolishly and insensitively blurted out to his family (Gen. 37:2–11). He could never have imagined the manner in which that dream would reach its fulfilment! He could never have worked that out himself! It was a long, slow, sometimes painful unwinding of the cords of grace which eventually led him to the final purposes of God.

The reason for this, of course, is that God is not only concerned that we know his will. His relationship with us is not merely intellectual. That is the great mistake many young people with the benefit of a college or university education are likely to make. In later life we will look back on it with a sense of what buffoons we were to think that God was simply a great Mind with whom we had come in contact. God is, instead, concerned with our personal, spiritual, emotional development. That is why he so often takes his time with us, in order to fit us for the work he has planned.

God is not in a hurry. That is what you must learn. That is what you can learn from the exhortations in the Psalms to *wait for the Lord*. He has long ago prepared the good works in which he wants you to talk (Eph. 2:10). There is no need to panic or to be anxious. He is not only your Life-Planner. He is a Father; he knows what we need before we ask him; he has numbered the hairs on our heads! We, who lack the patience for such an enterprise, should learn to trust the all-knowing wisdom of God.

What is the basic problem we face when we come to consider our life calling? It is this. In many areas of life we find that the Bible gives us clear-cut direction. We are not to lie or steal. It is forbidden. These are universally applicable commands. There is no exception to them. We have little difficulty knowing how to put them into practice. But our difficulties begin to arise when God says: you *may* do this; you *may* enjoy that. In fact, it is much more difficult to follow positive commands than negative ones (a fact we often fail to grasp when we think about the goodness of God in giving the commandments). For we are now faced with a choice! We may get married, for example. But (at least at first sight) there seem to be so many possibilities! We may work; but of all the multitude of occupations which are open to us, how are we to know the one to which God has called us?

There is no text in the Bible which tells you: *This is what you are to do with your life*. There are texts which say: *These are things which you must not do*. How then are we to arrive at the personal knowledge of God's will? There are several very important considerations.

(i) *Mark out the possibilities*

If you were to read through a careers manual, you would probably feel that the choice was so large that it might prove impossible. But it is not so. For one thing, all of us are able to limit the possibilities. It is always a wise course to try to do that.

There are some callings which are not legitimate for the Christian. Just as there are some people whom a Christian will refrain from marrying because it would be impossible to share life at the deepest level of faith in Christ with them, there are some callings in contemporary society which every Christian will regard as illegitimate. In fact it may well be to this rather than to the issue of marriage that the well-known passage in 2 Corinthians 6:14ff refers.

Immediately then, we have, however slightly, narrowed the field. Our aim will be, with God's help, to narrow down the field as far as possible.

(ii) *Consider your gifts*

This should provide a major help to discovering God's will. The God who is the Provider of the circumstances and opportunities of my life is also the Creator, who has made and fashioned me and given me the abilities and gifts I possess. He will not normally contradict his providences by his gifts. Rather he delights to match them together, and to watch his children's joy when they begin to realise how perfectly he has done so.

This principle governs the life and fellowship of the church. 'Having gifts that differ according to the grace given to us, let us use them', says Paul (Rom. 12:6 R.S.V.). But that principle will also govern the entire life of the believer. Some of us have natural gifts which tend to be intellectual; others are gifted in communicating with people; some gifts tend to be social in their application, others individual. Some are gifted by physical constitution, *as well as natural temperament*, for manual labour. What we should all be learning as the children of God is that, since he has made us, and loves us; since for the sake of the Lord Christ he accepts us as we are in order to transform us into his image, we must learn to accept ourselves and the opportunities and gifts God has given us. We must use them all for him.

We must beware of being covetous of others and their circumstances. It is sometimes sadly true that the real problem we may face in coming to know the Lord's will for our lives is that we have difficulty in accepting ourselves. We want to be different from what God has created us to be. But it is in acceptance that peace, and therefore usefulness, lies.

The presence of some gift in our life does not mean that we have a *right* to use it. There may be good reasons why the Giver does not want us to (he is more interested in producing graces than gifts). But, other things being equal, we should anticipate that God will want to use all that he has invested in our creation in the work to which he calls us. This is how John Murray expressed it:

> What path of life each individual is to follow in reference to this basic interest of life [i.e. his daily work] is to be determined by the proper gift which God has bestowed, and this is the index to the divine will and therefore the divine call.[1]

It is often at this juncture that we will find we need counsel and encouragement. For we are not all equally able to recognise our own natural and spiritual gifts. Some of us may also be in danger of burying them. Like the foolish man in Jesus' parable we reason like this: 'I have only one gift, unlike my friends. There is no real point in my trying to use it. I am never going to have a great influence like my friends. I will just bury it.' So, it will help us considerably to share our concern with some Christian of greater experience.

Perhaps your natural reaction is: 'I could never go and ask someone what they thought of my gifts, just like that'. I appreciate your difficulty. But perhaps your motives are not all that they should be. At times what we call 'modesty' is really a cross between pride

[1] John Murray, *Principles of Conduct*, 1957, p. 86.

and a lack of commitment to the will of God. If we are in earnest about knowing the Lord's will, we shall very much want humbly to share our concerns with one or two trusted Christian friends. When we ourselves are older, looking back we shall realise that often our minister, or elder was much more conscious of our gifts and possible usefulness than we could ever have been. Would it be too bitter a pill for you to swallow to recognise that even your parents might have learned something about your pattern of life over all the years they have nourished you? That is why the Book of Proverbs gives us such wise counsel as this: 'The way of a fool seems right to him, but a wise man listens to advice' (Prov. 12:15).

Few verses are more frequently quoted in connection with God's guidance than Isaiah 30:21: 'Whether you turn to the right or to the left, your ears will hear a voice behind you, saying, "This is the way; walk in it".' What is too frequently ignored is the immediate context, which suggests that the voice is not the inner voice of the Spirit, acting like a rudder for the believer; it is the voice of one of our 'teachers' (Is. 30:20). It is through their counsel that God regularly enables us to discover his will! 'Plans fail for lack of counsel, but with many advisers they succeed' (Prov. 15:22).

(iii) *Consider the needs*

This too must have priority for the Christian. For he does not live to himself. His work is in the service of God. It is not merely a way of earning money, or of pleasing himself. Since his chief duties are to love God and to love his neighbour as himself, he will place *need* before *reward* when he considers the possible paths he may take.

Have you asked the question: What needs are there which my life might help to meet? Often, when candidates for service in overseas missions are interviewed, one of the questions they will be asked is: What do you know of the needs? There are many reasons for that question. It brings to the surface the extent to which a 'call' is a reflection of a God-given concern. A sense of some pressing need is sometimes a good indication that the Lord has been shaping the direction of our lives to help to meet it. Of course, there are exceptions (Jonah was called to Nineveh when he seemed to have little or no sense of the real need of grace the people had). But they *are* exceptions. More commonly God works according to the pattern he used in the experience of Isaiah, who was conscious of his own and his people's needs, and so responded: 'Here am I. Send me!'

No Christian today should be able to avoid the need of the world for the message of the gospel. Certainly many Christians should seriously ask God whether the work of the regular ministry or the work of evangelism overseas might be his will for their lives. R. L. Dabney's words still ring true more than a century after they were written:

> Go where we may, we see more merchants than can find customers, more physicians than have patients, more lawyers than clients. Society has enough of them – too many. But . . . to carry the gospel to every one of the 800 millions of pagans on our globe, the church needs a hundred times as many ministers. Now, what young Christian, qualified to preach, who asks in the spirit of the true convert 'Lord, what wilt thou have me to do?' can say in view of these facts, that *God and his fellow men have more need of him at the bar, behind the counter, or in the physician's calling, than in the pulpit?* If he cannot, let him

beware how he neglects the prayerful examination of the duty of preaching, at the peril of the wrath of his Saviour.[1]

It has sometimes been said in recent times that the need of the world constitutes the call. That is a great mistake. It is a mistake which R. L. Dabney very carefully guards against in these words. There is no evidence that this was the all-governing principle in the teaching of the apostles; nor has it been so at any period of the church's life. To have Christians engaged in full-time ministry or the work of overseas evangelism who were neither called nor gifted for it would be tragic. But, *many more Christians ought to be looking their Saviour in the face to tell him: 'Here am I. Send me!' We have too few who are willing to put into practice their profession to leave all for the sake of Christ.* There is great need in the church and in the world. We cannot afford to turn a blind eye to it.

There may also be needs at home which will help to shut us in to the will of God. Our immediate family situation may circumscribe our lives. There are duties which we are bound by God to treat as primary concerns. Honouring our father and mother, visiting the fatherless and the widow – these may greatly limit where we are able to go and what we are enabled to do in life. Our responsibilities, according to Paul, extend to grandparents too. If God calls us to such a ministry of love and mercy, we must ask his help to seal in our consciences the assurance that being in the centre of his will, however mundane and trying it seems, is the safest, and ultimately the happiest place in the world.

We must learn too to take a long-term view. One of my most gifted friends told me once how he had discovered, to his great surprise, that as a young man

[1] R. L. Dabney, *Discussions Evangelical and Theological* (Banner of Truth edition), vol 2, 1967, p. 41.

his father had been preparing to go to China as a missionary. His father had then died suddenly, and it became absolutely necessary for him to remain at home. He gave the whole of his life to secular work which might even have seemed mundane to the son who knew nothing of the father's secret for many years. But what others could see were the unusual gifts which the father had prayed down from heaven on his son. God was working his purpose out in the son's life in a way which would probably have been impossible had the father become a missionary. The story could be paralleled many times, in many lives. We do not live or die to ourselves, but to the Lord and his will. He understands what he is doing. If at first sight he narrows the possibilities for our lives to the very mundane, we can trust him. If we are faithful in that which we think to be least, he will not be our debtor.

At times there will be a conflict of interests and loyalties. I remember reading a very sad letter in an evening newspaper which illustrated this. The writer was a mother whose daughter was about to leave home as a missionary. Was there nobody who could tell the daughter that she was wasting her life? Had the mother not done everything for her, and was this the reward she received? Painful enough to leave home! More painful still for our 'calling' to be resented! But it can and does happen. It will lead to great heart-searching on our part if it does. Are we truly in the Lord's will? Are we following his commands, or are we, perhaps, running from his will because even overseas life might prove to be easier than life with the people among whom God has set us? Those who return with joy, having reaped the harvest, may well be those who have gone with costly weeping, against such a background. The will of the Lord for sinners in a sinful world is not always straightforward. It is not guaranteed to be easy. It must always, ultimately, be costly.

(iv) *Consider your personal desires*

'Delight yourself in the Lord and he will give you the desires of your heart' (Ps. 37:4).

> *Hast thou not seen*
> *How thy heart's wishes have been*
> *Granted in what he ordaineth?*

None the less, many Christians retain a deep-seated suspicion of God and his desire to bless us. There is something written into the sinful heart which, from the time of the Fall, has regarded God as less than beneficent, less than generous and spontaneously loving to his children.

The subtle innuendo of the serpent in the Garden of Eden was: 'Surely God has hedged your life around with all these petty restrictions'. Are we afraid to believe his word when it assures us: 'he will give you the desires of your heart'? How often we are like the one-talent man who said to his master: 'I knew that you are a hard man . . . So I was afraid and went out and hid your talent in the ground. See, here is what belongs to you' (Matt. 25:24–5)! We do not really believe that God has a loving purpose for us.

We will never come to know and enjoy the will of the Lord, and find it good, perfect and acceptable until we first gain a true view of God and his fatherly character towards us. Here again is how John Murray put it:

There is no conflict between the gratification of desire and the enhancement of man's pleasure, on the one hand, and fulfilment of God's command on the other . . . The tension

87

that often exists within us between a sense of duty and wholehearted spontaneity is a tension that arises from sin and a disobedient will. No such tension would have invaded the heart of unfallen man. And the operations of saving grace are directed to the end of removing the tension so that there may be, as there was with man at the beginning, the perfect complementation of duty and pleasure, of commandment and love.[1]

Our desires on their own are not trustworthy. But at the same time, taken along with other considerations, they may point us in the direction of the service for which God has created us. This is true, for example, of the call to Christian service. It is also, by extension, true of every sphere in which we seek to honour Christ. Consequently the New Testament is able to speak about men in these terms: 'If anyone sets his heart on becoming an overseer, he desires a noble task' (1 Tim. 3:1). The verb Paul uses (*oregō*) means 'to reach out to touch' something. That desire, Paul is saying, is not sinful or illegitimate. It is not necessarily proud and self-seeking. It may well be God-given, and it should be recognised as a gift from him if it is so.

If a sphere of work and service is God's will for us, we should expect that, in a similar way, some measure of aspiration for it will develop in our hearts. It may take a period of time to emerge in our conscious thinking, and a longer time to dawn on us that this really is the will of God. Of course we will need to ask him to rid us of all impure motivation. But if we are altogether lacking in motivation, equally indifferent to all spheres of service, careless of whether *this* or *that* will be more glorifying to God in our lives, it is unlikely that the will of God means anything vital to us at all.

We are faced with a momentous decision when we

[1] *Op. cit.* p. 39.

commit ourselves to a life calling. In God's mercy we do not know the full extent of the decision we are taking. As we look back in later years we may confess that if we had known, we would have been paralysed with fear, and done nothing. But God has promised grace which is sufficient for our needs. He will guard his children in their decisions. He will not let our feet slip. He loves his children; he loves their obedience. He will prosper the work of their hands.

Consider your gifts. Consider the needs. Consider your settled interests and desires.

> In all your ways acknowledge him,
>   and he will make your paths straight.

Proverbs 3:6

7: *Marriage?*

HAS the time come for you, as it comes to most of us, when one of the questions about the will of God which lies most heavily on your mind is: Does the Lord wish me to get married? Men and women adopt very different attitudes and approaches to this question. They do so because of those distinctive differences which God has implanted in male and female, but also because of different needs, desires, circumstances and upbringing among those of the same sex. Yet, there is clearly something so fundamental about the unique relationship involved in marriage that every Christian is likely to consider it at some stage in life.

Most of us have some close friends who have not yet married, and may never do so. Time will tell. But why have they retained their single status? They are eligible, spiritual, attractive in personality and features, yet they remain unmarried! Why should this be?

We do not always know what proposals may have been made or received and rejected. There may be disappointed hopes in some hearts. But one thing is sure for the obedient child of God. A single state is to be pursued so long as it is the will of God. That is why our single friends, who may have had one or more opportunities to marry, remain single as obedient Christians. They believe that the Lord has thus planned it.

But this is no less true of those who marry. It is one of the great joys of being part of a Christian fellowship to share in the pleasure of those who have given their hearts to each other because they see that as the way of obedience to the Lord. What is so moving is the discovery that our own natural aspirations and the will of God should meet at such a point!

How, then, are we to assess the situation for ourselves? How do we know what is God's will for us? We have already seen that God's normal way of leading his people is by their application of biblical principles to personal circumstances. It may be that as you are reading these pages you are already head-over-heels in love with somebody. That is certainly a circumstance! It is also partly a biological condition. It is not in itself a biblical principle, and your immediate task is to bring to bear on these circumstances, and on your natural feelings, the great principles of God's word.

Two principles in particular will bring stability to those who find themselves asking heart-searching questions in this area. This chapter is written with them in mind. But it is a healthy exercise for those who may be older and well into married life to remember the principles on which our most important human friendships are based. The two principles are these: 1. *Be realistic in your expectations*. 2. *Be biblical in your preparation*. We shall examine the first briefly, and the second at greater length.

1. *Be Realistic in Your Expectations*

There are several levels at which this is sound advice. We should, for example, remember that angels do not marry, nor are they given in marriage (Matt. 22:30). We are fallen creatures, tainted in every area of our lives, mentally, spiritually, physically, by the effects of the Fall. Marriage, and the process of coming to it, is not heaven! It is the bonding together of two needy sinners in order to make a partnership which is substantially greater than either of them alone. Marriage will not answer all our problems. It may show us, through the intense closeness of the relationship, problems which we did not know we had. Our marriage partner will not become perfect simply by the act of marriage! Nor should we make the mistake of thinking that marriage will provide the ultimate satisfaction for which we all hunger. To assume so would be to be guilty of blasphemy. Only God satisfies the hungry heart. Marriage is but one of the channels he uses to enable us to taste how deeply satisfying his thirst-quenching grace can be.

Furthermore, we do well to recognise that courtship will not necessarily be a smooth process simply because we are Christians. Some of the roughest courtships result in the most happy and fruitful marriages. It would be a foolish Christian who wanted to stereotype the mystery of two young (or old) people finding that only together could they be fully in God's will. Sometimes it may even be that difficulties seem to increase because in the case of Christians there is a spiritual dimension in courtship, a wrestling with the will of God, which is totally absent in the case of others. Furthermore, if a partnership is going to prove to be fruitful in the future, we can be sure that the devil will leave nothing undone in order to mar or destroy it in its earliest stages.

Again, we should not expect that Christians will all follow the same path to the day of their marriage. Scripture furnishes us with a sufficient number of illustrations to indicate that there will be great diversity in this. Not everyone will be like Isaac who met his wife in the middle of his evening devotions! (See Gen. 24:63ff.) Nor will every courtship follow the stormy pattern of the Lover and the Maiden in the Song of Solomon. It is paradoxical that *this* courtship should be seen as an allegory of the marriage of Christ and his church by some Christians who would stereotype Christian courtship to as tranquil an experience as possible! 'Do not let it upset you' is their motto! But for some, discovering a deep and lasting need for someone else's companionship can be one of the most traumatic experiences in life. At such a time all kinds of assumptions about ourselves may be reversed dramatically. The process of coming to see ourselves and our future in a new light is often a most perturbing thing.

Another dimension of such realism can be expressed in this way. If we are to marry, only God can bring us to the person we are to marry. If, once we are married, we are able to look back on the intricacies involved in bringing together two such diverse people as we are, we will wonder why we did not more totally trust our Heavenly Father. If everything, including the day of our birth, the nature of our upbringing, the circumstances of our lives and a thousand and one other details, is afterwards seen to be in the sovereign control of God, we can surely be realistic beforehand and trust him in the assurance that he always knows what is best. *Be realistic in your Christian life!*

2. *Be Biblical in Your Preparation*

No book on marriage will give you a marriage partner. A chapter like this in a book on guidance will not reduce by a single degree the necessity for you to go through the experience of discovering the will of God for your own life. This point needs to be emphasised. The very fact that you are reading a book on guidance may indicate that you feel in need of it in certain areas of your life. You are asking questions and looking for answers. But no book on guidance on earth can answer your questions the way you would like them answered. The only thing others can offer you is the wisdom of Scripture and the assurance of its truth and reliability in experience. You must discover that for yourself. But, there are principles enshrined in Scripture which will give stability, safety and wisdom to you as you contemplate the prospect, or possibility, of marriage. *What are these principles?* There are five of them, and they can be cast in the form of questions which might be used to help us to discern the Lord's will.

1. *What is Marriage for?* We too readily overlook this fundamental question. Yet we would ask it in almost every other area of life. Only when we have some appreciation of the purpose of the marriage relationship are we likely to discern God's will in particular instances. Similarly, when we see that purpose, we will immediately recognise that there will be a restricted range of even our best friends with whom it would be possible to fulfil it.

Marriage was originally given by God because he was concerned to overcome man's loneliness in the world (Gen. 2:18). None of the members of the animal kingdom was able to supply the special fellowship which man needed (Gen. 2:20). So God fashioned the first woman, in order to provide *fellowship* for Adam. It was, in one sense, as simple and uncomplicated as that. The powerful sexual drives which are built in to man's relationship with woman are not seen in Scripture as the foundation of marriage, but the consummation and physical expression of it. Marriage is first and foremost to provide what our contemporary jargon calls 'togetherness'.

When this is appreciated it gives rise to a series of questions which become particularly important when I contemplate marriage: Is my friend (girl, boy) the kind of person to whom I could give such fellowship, and from whom I would receive it? Are we really suited to one another at this level? At the most basic level, inevitably, I must ask questions about the mutual strength of our spiritual interests and concerns. But at other levels I must ask whether the interests we have in common, the tastes, backgrounds, experiences, general outlooks are such that we will find enrichment where we have common ground *and* where our predispositions are very different. When some chemicals are mixed in the laboratory a new and valuable compound may be formed. On the other hand, there may be a reaction which produces an explosion! Christian marriage is a gift from God to create a new kind of fellowship, a more creative entity than would be possible otherwise.

Am I preparing myself to be such a partner? Is the person to whom I am presently drawn and attracted suited to me, and *vice versa*, in this way?

2. *What should I look for in a husband or wife?* Scripture provides some important insights into the different expectations which men and women will have in seeking a marriage partner. Today, our society has eroded these biblical distinctions. It has undercut the biblical teaching that these differences are built into our creation. The great scriptural emphases need constant repetition. Men and women are different, not as the result of cultural pressures, nor because of accidents of evolution. They are different because God

made them so. *He made them male and female* (Gen. 1:27).

Because these fundamental differences exist, in physical dimensions, general cast of mind and approach to situations, strengths and needs, men and women will generally look for different things in marriage. Scripture recognises this.

When Ruth looked to Boaz to marry her, she described her wish in these terms: 'Spread the corner of your garment over me . . .' (Ruth 3:9). The word which our versions translate 'garment' here means 'wing'. It is, significantly, the same word which Boaz had earlier used when he spoke to Ruth: 'May you be richly rewarded by the Lord, the God of Israel, under whose *wings* you have come to take refuge' (Ruth 2:12). Having found protection under God's wings, she now seeks protection under those of Boaz!

In a Christian marriage there will always be an element of this. That is not to say, necessarily, that an unmarried lady is poor, weak and defenceless! But it does suggest that within the marriage relationship a woman will become conscious of needs, weaknesses, a desire for the protecting company of her husband in a way she did not before marriage. Is it not significant that Ruth had already been married? She was now without the 'wings' of a husband to protect her.

When I contemplate marriage, therefore, these thoughts will be at the back of my mind as I seek God's best: Is this the kind of man who will provide such protecting fellowship when areas of my need are exposed through the very experience of marriage? Is this girl someone that I would give my very life to shield from harm and danger? Romantic chivalry is but a pale reflection of Christian marriage!

Another aspect of this is emphasised in the creation

narratives. What God wanted to give to man was a *help-meet*. The word seems to convey the idea of someone who is suited to him, in whom he recognises himself. That is a profound insight. It reflects the discoveries so many Christians make in marriage. A man will discover himself, and will rise to a new stature through the fellowship and ministry of the woman he loves.

This is by no stretch of the imagination to imply a lack of growth in those who are single. To suggest that would be to impugn the *perfect* humanity of Jesus. Single men and women are not inadequate! The only point being made is that marriage creates a new dimension *in those who marry*. It brings out their full potential in a way that nothing else can do.

Is that what happens to me, in some measure, with the girl with whom I am contemplating marriage? Do I see, again in some measure, that the young man with whom I have become so friendly is *growing* through our relationship? Or, is he shrinking because of it?

3. *How do we fulfil the different roles of husband and wife?* When Paul addresses himself to the doctrine of marriage in Ephesians 5:21–33, he does so on the basis of a universal principle. Christians are to exercise mutual submission to one another out of their reverence for Christ.

Mutual submission exists within marriage. For mutual submission, in this context, means primarily to yield to the best interests of others. But, notice that *Paul's application of this principle is different for husbands and wives*. The role of the wife is to submit to her husband as the head of her life. That is, in turn, different from the general mutual submission Paul had mentioned in the previous verse. It is a specific submission to God-given authority (not a suppressing of one's general rights for the sake of others). The wife will do this out of reverence for Christ, because he has constituted family life in this way. Just as all Christians are to submit to Christ as their head, so wives give an illustration of this in their relationship to their husbands.

On the other hand, the husband is also to consider his wife. He is to love and cherish her; he is to sacrifice himself for her just as Christ did for his bride the church. Either task demands a life of sacrifice. Both are rooted in the principle of obedience to Christ as Lord.

Without this biblical balance marriage partners are forced apart. A home needs leadership and a source for its authority. A husband without the loving submission of his wife will find himself the head of an unhappy home. The wife who is not loved with sacrificial, self-giving love will either lose her personality or become something of a nag!

Now, the fundamental question is: Is this the kind of man or woman for whom I have the respect which is the foundation of love? Can I respect him so fully that I would want, with God's help, to be this kind of wife? Is this the kind of lady to whom, with God's help, I would be able to give a Christ-like love? Are these my motives?

4. *What is the character of marriage?* I am not only contemplating a new relationship with someone. I am contemplating a new status for both of us. What is involved in this new status?

The Lord Jesus Christ stamped his own authority on the words of Genesis 2:24 in this connection: 'For this reason a man will leave his father and mother and be united to his wife, and they will become one flesh'. Three features of the marital status are thus summarised. *It is exclusive.* A man quits his former status at home, and *leaves* his parents. Incidentally, that may mean that we should think very seriously before marrying when we are in no position to leave our parents. At best, residence with in-laws should be a temporary expedient! More important is the element implied in these words that our status in relationship to our parents is altered. While we continue to honour them in accordance with God's commandment, our marriage partner now has priority.

Marriage is not only an exclusive relationship. *It is permanent*. The man is united to his wife. He 'cleaves' to her. Marriage is a life-long commitment. It demands a commitment of the mind, the will, the affections, everything! That is why it is such a powerful illustration of conversion to Christ (Eph. 5:32).

Marriage is also a *creative* relationship, as we have already seen. The two become one! What could be more mysterious? Yet, two become one in this instance, not by division, but by multiplication. When Genesis says that God made woman for the man, the verb it uses is one which would be used of building a house. Some of the Jewish rabbis believed that this had something to do with the woman's shape. Ideas of beauty change! Clearly what is meant is that the woman became the *home* for the man; she living under his protection, he dwelling in her love and welcome. This *is* marriage.

But is this the marriage we contemplate? Again we discover that there is always an element of *the consecration of our will* in God's leading, as well as *a discovery and understanding of his will*.

You may have a special friendship. But is *it* capable of this quality of devotion and commitment? Are *you* capable of that kind of consecration within it?

5. *What is the ultimate aim of marriage?* When God made

'man', he made him male and female, in his own image (Gen. 1:27). It is impossible to be dogmatic about the precise significance of these words. But they do seem to contain a suggestion that it is man-and-woman, not merely humanity, which reflects the image of God. Here, in the marriage relationship, there can exist a pale, but real reflection of the social fellowship within God's own Being as Father, Son and Holy Spirit.

The ultimate aim of marriage is to reflect God's image; to reflect the glory of his grace and Being. This means that *marriage can never be an end in itself*. It exists for a greater purpose than its own fulfilment.

When two people are joined in the Lord, something of the glory of God should be seen. The Father's love for his Son; the Son's love for his Father; the Spirit's love for both – these should be at least sensed and tasted in a Christian marriage. If there is grace in it, then there will be a touch of glory in it too. God demonstrated his glory most clearly in the sacrifice of his Son. So a marriage demonstrates the glory of God when at its heart there is a spirit of self-sacrificing love.

Is that my aim? Our aim, as we contemplate life together? Do we sense that God will make this possible? Do others recognise that our relationship has something of the image and glory of God in it? Can I pray, as Temple Gairdner did before his wedding:

That I may come nearer to her,
Draw me nearer to Thee than to her;
That I may know her, make me to know Thee
  more than her;
That I may love her, with the perfect love of a
  perfectly whole heart
Cause me to love Thee more than her, and most of
  all.

The ability to pray like that may be the clearest sign of all, that God has purposed and will bring to pass what we contemplate.

How, then, do we respond to these issues? They should help us to clarify our minds about many vital matters. They may put brakes on relationships we might otherwise have begun or continued. But, in the last analysis, they are only helps, aids, tests, by which we may discern the Lord's will. They will not bring to us the gift of marriage. That gift is available only from the Lord himself. From him we should ask for it, if it be his will; in his word we should find the wisdom we shall need to discern the purpose of his grace; by the earnest prayer of a humble, God-fearing heart, and the consistent application of his truth to our circumstances, he will not let our foot be moved. He will keep us (Ps. 121:3).

8: *Wait for the Lord*

When you picked up this book and began to read it you may have been interested in a very general way in the subject of knowing God's will. It is a subject in which every Christian has an interest. Alternatively, you may have been attracted to these pages because you have a specific need for guidance. You are wanting to know what you should do *now*. You have been hoping that, as you read, your own problem will be resolved. Indeed, that may have happened! But it is possible that it has not. You really hoped for more, even although you would agree that there is no book written which could guarantee to give you the answers for which you are searching. Perhaps you are a little disappointed. What can you do now?

Quite often those who find they are faced with difficulties about the Lord's will are advised to read certain booklets, or given advice passed on from others. Sometimes they reply: 'I read it' or 'I know that', 'but it didn't help me'. Few answers cut would-be counsellors so brutally down to size, especially if they themselves have found great help in either the book or the wise advice. But, sensitive counsellors will also hear warning bells sound when we respond in this way. Almost invariably such a reply seems to be saying: 'My problem, my needs, my gifts, my circumstances are all too complex, too unusual for *that* kind of counsel'. It is never a healthy sign for a Christian to be convinced that he has a problem which nobody else could have or fully understand. For such people, there is a final word of biblical counsel. It has a wide application and is relevant to every Christian who longs to know the will of God. It is the one word: WAIT! Wait for the Lord!

The book of Lamentations gives us an example of this principle. In the context of an experience of suffering, sorrow and difficulty, words are spoken which apply whenever the unfolding of God's purposes seems to be delayed:

The Lord is good to those whose hope is in him,
    to the one who seeks him;
It is good to wait quietly
    for the salvation of the Lord.
It is good for a man to bear the yoke
    while he is young.

Let him sit alone in silence,
    for the Lord has laid it on him.
Let him bury his face in the dust –
    there may yet be hope.
Let him offer his cheek to one who would strike him,
    and let him be filled with disgrace.

For men are not cast off
    by the Lord for ever.
Though he brings grief, he will show compassion,
    so great is his unfailing love.
For he does not willingly bring affliction
    or grief to the children of men.

Lamentations 3:25–33

Here we find an abundance of lessons. These are lessons which should be learned in youth, we are told. Something in us needs to be broken then, so that, like Jacob, having met with God, we walk with the marks of our submission to him for the rest of our lives (Gen. 32:22–32). If *impatience* is not subdued then, it may remain like a wild animal in our hearts until it can never be fruitfully tamed. What a strange paradox it is that the Lord does not willingly afflict us, and yet he does a work through our 'disgrace' – our burying our face in the dust – which can be done in no other way. Sometimes, when the will of the Lord is not plain to us, there is an element of this divine purpose in God's overruling of our affairs. It is part of his working everything together for good for those who have in their hearts a genuine love for him and his kingdom (Rom. 8:28).

These words in Lamentations could easily have been penned by Joseph, for this was God's way of dealing with him. He was a young man of unusual abilities, destined to be greatly used by God. But impatience would have been his ruin, had not God begun to deal with his character at a deep and very painful level. Through all the vicissitudes of his life in Egypt he learned to wait in silence for God. Impatience was slain. He became willing to wait.

The biblical vocabulary for waiting on God is very rich and full. It conveys various nuances of the spiritual disciplines involved in discovering the purposes of God in our lives.

We are to wait on the Lord *in the sense of being silent before him*. So the Psalmist testifies in Psalm 62:1, 5:

My soul finds rest in God alone;
my salvation comes from him.

Find rest, O my soul, in God alone;
my hope comes from him.

The word translated 'rest' in the *New International Version* really means '*to be silent*'. 'My soul waiteth in silence for God only' (A.S.V.). It is the recognition that we lack wisdom, and must depend on God alone for it, that is being expressed. Waiting on God, in this sense, lies at the heart of the Christian's experience. We cannot become Christians, and confess 'my salvation comes from him', without learning this awed silence before God.

No-one has expressed this more pointedly than Dr D. M. Lloyd-Jones did in his exposition of Paul's argument that, because of sin, every mouth must be shut and the whole world held guilty before God (Rom. 3:19):

> How do you know whether a man is a Christian? The answer is that his mouth is 'shut'. I like this forthrightness of the Gospel. People need to have their mouths shut, 'stopped'. They are for ever talking about God, and criticizing God, and pontificating about what God should or should not do, and asking 'Why does God allow this and that?' You do not begin to be a Christian until your mouth is shut, is stopped, and you are speechless and have nothing to say.[1]

That is not a spirit which is put behind us as we grow in grace. It is an abiding principle. We are always sinners before a holy God; finite sinners before God's eternal and infinite glory. Who are we to answer back to God? (Rom. 9:20) Let us seek the humility to be silent before him. 'Stand still, and wait for God!' This too is the message of Lamentations 3:25 to us.

[1] D. M. Lloyd-Jones, Romans: *Atonement and Justification*, 1970, p. 19.

We are also to wait on God *in the sense of doing so trustingly*. Psalm 37:7 teaches us:

Be still before the Lord and wait patiently for him;
  do not fret when men succeed in their ways,
  when they carry out their wicked schemes.

The context is that of the apparent success of evil and the relative failure and poverty of the good. We do not see that there is obvious blessing in trusting that God will reveal his will. We see others, who have turned from God's ways, succeed. Then we begin to fret. We become anxious. We become impatient. If we do not take matters into our own hands, the prosperity we seek (and believe God has promised) will have slipped out of our grasp – so we reason!

But God's counsel is: Wait! Do not fret! So the Psalmist continues:

Do not fret – it leads only to evil.
For evil men will be cut off,
but those who hope in the Lord will inherit the land.

Consequently, we are to wait on the Lord, *in a spirit of expectation*. We speak colloquially of the period when a mother-to-be is carrying her child and waiting for the little one to be born, as the months when she is 'expecting' her baby. It is not always an easy time; there may be discomfort, sickness and a little anxiety. It is sometimes much more tiring to be expecting the baby than looking after it! Yet the waiting is suffused with a spirit of anticipation. So it is with the child of God as he waits on his Father's will.

The word which is translated 'wait' in Psalm 37:7 originally seems to have carried the idea of twisting or writhing. It conveys a sense of the intensity which can be involved in this waiting on God. It is not a passive tranquillity, by any manner of means. It means *to be on the stretch*. Waiting on God, being silent before him, may involve a protracted battle with the world, the flesh and the devil!

These, then, are some of the characteristics of waiting for God. It will be obvious that they conflict with many of our natural dispositions and aspirations. It may therefore be a helpful thing to bring out into the open some of the real difficulties we have in entering into the rest of faith to which we are invited by God.

Our Difficulties

(1) We are reluctant to accept our status in this world as *pilgrims*. God has set in our hearts a desire for a city which has lasting foundations (Heb. 11:10). But we have a sinful predisposition to put down roots in the city of the world rather than the city of God. Because of that we have a tendency to want the certainty and freedom *in this world* which is inappropriate to those who are aliens in it and working, as it were, on a temporary visa. *Not knowing* is one of life's greatest anxieties. It is particularly excruciating when, for example, we are waiting the results of medical tests or treatment. The same spirit inevitably spills over into our general Christian experience. We find that the burden of waiting without knowing is more than we can bear. Sometimes as a result we anxiously try to force God's hand. We become like the Israelites who consistently reacted against their pilgrim life:

> But they soon forgot what he had done
> and did not wait for his counsel.

107

In the desert they gave in to their craving;
   in the wasteland they put God to the test.
So he gave them what they asked for,
   but sent a wasting disease upon them.

Psalm 106:13–15

Many a promising Christian life has been paralysed because of a failure to deal with this cause of impatience before God.

(2) We are sometimes unwilling to bow to the sovereign providences of God in our lives. We become bitter against him, and consequently refuse to wait for his leading. We become frustrated with God.

Sometimes this spirit is disguised, or diverted. Instead of openly criticising God for the way in which he works, we divert that opposition to others – our friends, the circumstances in which we find ourselves, or the failures and sins of the church to which we belong. But all the while there is eating into our soul a bitterness against what God has done.

There was an element of this in Job's reaction to God. He quite rightly contended that he was not suffering because he had sinned (the opening chapters of the book reveal that he actually suffered because of his righteous life; rather than being punished by God, it was Satan who had demanded to have him, to sift him like wheat). But his bitter experience did unveil a measure of the remaining corruption of his heart. He began to contend with the Almighty (Job 40:2). In God's grace he learned to put his hand over his mouth (Job 40:4), to confess:

I know that you can do all things;
no plan of yours can be thwarted.
. . .

Surely I spoke of things I did not understand,
things too wonderful for me to know.

. . .

My ears had heard of you
   but now my eyes have seen you.
Therefore I despise myself
   and repent in dust and ashes.

Job 42:2–6

Do you need to know more of this spirit, as you wait upon God? Is there an unwillingness on your part to accept his will? Is that why you are not discovering that his yoke is easy and his burden light? Is that why you know so little of what it means to 'find rest' in the Lord?

We need to learn to breathe the spirit of Psalm 123:

I lift my eyes to you,
   to you whose throne is in heaven.
As the eyes of slaves look to the hand of
   their master,
as the eyes of a maid look to the hand of
   her mistress,
so our eyes look to the Lord our God,
   till he shows us his mercy.

(3) We lack faith in the goodness of God. There is built into every sinner a suspicion of God. The opening chapters of the Bible describe how it was planted into our first parents by the tempter. He deceived and seduced the minds of God's children; he distorted their view of God and cast doubts into their minds about his goodness: 'Did God say you were not to eat of any of the trees in the garden?' The prohibition of *one* tree,

Satan insinuated, is the prohibition of all joy, all freedom. 'If you are ever to be free – like God himself is free – you must eat!'

All impatience can be traced back to a disbelief in God's ultimate goodness. That is why, if we are to appreciate the wisdom of God's guidance, it is important for us to understand not only the nature of his guidance, but the character of the Guide himself. Trust him for his goodness, and we will trust him for his guidance!

Do you doubt the goodness of God? *Is there, lurking within your whole approach to him, a suspicion that he is other than he revealed himself to be in the Lord Jesus Christ?* Hold to Paul's words:

> He who did not spare his own Son, but gave him up for us all – how will he not also, along with him, graciously give us all things?
>
> Romans 8:32

(4) We are too easily influenced by the attitudes of the age in which we live. The clamour today is for the immediate, not for the long-term and the lasting. Nor has the church escaped. Evangelical Christianity, for all its profession to believe in an eternal God and a future hope, has shown many distressing symptoms of a near-sighted, short-minded passion for the instant.

We need to heed the stirring words of A. W. Tozer. Writing on the theme of 'The Inadequacy of Instant Christianity', he said this:

> Instant Christianity tends to make the faith act terminal and so smothers the desire for spiritual advance. It fails to understand the true nature of the Christian life, which is not static but dynamic and expanding. It overlooks the fact that a new Christian is a living organism as certainly

as a new baby is, and must have nourishment and exercise to assure normal growth. It does not consider that the act of faith in Christ sets up a personal relationship between two intelligent moral beings, God and the reconciled man, and no single encounter between God and a creature made in his image could ever be sufficient to establish an intimate friendship between them.

By trying to pack all of salvation into one experience, or two, the advocates of instant Christianity flaunt the law of development which runs through all nature. They ignore the sanctifying effects of suffering, cross carrying and practical obedience. They pass by the need for spiritual training, the necessity of forming right religious habits and the need to wrestle against the world, the devil and the flesh . . .

Instant Christianity is twentieth-century orthodoxy. I wonder whether the man who wrote Philippians 3:7–16 would recognise it as the faith for which he finally died. I am afraid he would not.[1]

God is not in a hurry. He is a patient craftsman as he shapes lives into the image of his Son. He is prepared to wait. He knows there is all eternity for the finished item to be enjoyed. You and I must likewise turn aside from instant methods to knowing the will of God in the long term.

God is not unaware of our difficulties and anxieties. He perfectly understands us and our frailties. He is also willing to come to our aid. It would be quite wrong, then, if we looked only at the difficulties we may have to surmount without also considering the many encouragements he gives us to wait for him.

[1] A. W. Tozer, *That Incredible Christian*, 1964, pp. 24–5.

Divine Encouragements

When Lamentations 3:25ff was quoted earlier in this chapter, we discovered that the author had come to certain fundamental conclusions about the will of God in his life. The basis of those conclusions is to be found in the immediately preceding verses. There we discover that he had come to know, in the character of his Lord, the very encouragements which would enable him to wait patiently for God to show himself:

> Because of the Lord's great love we are not
>   consumed,
>   for his compassions never fail.
> They are new every morning;
>   great is your faithfulness.
> I say to myself, *'The Lord is my portion;*
>   *therefore I will wait for him.'*
>
> Lamentations 3:22–24

If only we remember whose we are, we shall find the strong encouragements of an all-sufficient God sustaining us as we wait on him. Two things in particular should be remembered:

God longs to bless his people. Isaiah 30:18 assures us that those who *wait for* the Lord will be blessed. In this context the word 'wait' means 'to tarry'. But this expression is also used of God in the same verse:

> The Lord longs [waits] to be gracious to you;
>   he rises to show you compassion.

God is waiting for us to wait for him! He is eager to extend to us the blessing of being drawn into his secret purposes for our lives. But so long as he sees us impatiently wandering in our own wilful directions he holds back from the special intimacy of revealing his covenant purposes for us. What else can we expect, when we will not entrust him with the guidance of our lives? We cannot receive what we refuse to trust him for.

The first encouragement to patient waiting that we are given, is the knowledge that to wait like this in expectation is to grow more like God himself. It is to become godly, and so to prove how good and perfect and acceptable God's will is. In such intimacy with the Lord, and reflection of his own character, lies untold blessing.

But there is another aspect of biblical teaching which should be recalled for our encouragement. *God has his own place and time to act. He has his purposes to fulfil in us as well as his will to reveal to us.* When the prophet Habakkuk was wrestling with the problem of the will of God in his society, it was in this knowledge that he learned patience:

I will stand at my watch
    and station myself on the ramparts;
I will look to see what he will say to me,
    and what answer I am to give to this complaint.

Then the Lord replied:

'Write down the revelation
    and make it plain on tablets
so that a herald may run with it.
For the revelation awaits an appointed time;
    it speaks of the end
    and will not prove false.
Though it linger, wait for it;
    it will certainly come and will not delay.'

Habakkuk 2:1–3

113

Appearances can be deceptive. The fact that we cannot see what God is doing does not mean that he is doing nothing. The Lord has his own timetable. It is we who must learn to adjust to it, not *vice versa*. When God's time comes nothing will stand in his way. We can therefore wait for him with this happy confidence: 'As for God, his way is perfect' (2 Sam. 22:31).

Jesus lived in this confidence. He submitted his life to the timetable which God had appointed. He had to wait with patience during the days when his 'time was not yet come'.

God also has his purposes to fulfil *in us*. He is much more deeply concerned with our lives than we think. His will is to be worked in us, not only shown to us. His aim is our sanctification – that we should be living exemplifications of his will. That is why he calls us to endure, in order that patience may be wrought into our characters (Rom. 5:3–4; Jas. 1:3–4). For all the time we are walking according to his revealed will he is preparing and equipping us for the fulfilment of his secret will and purpose.

Take Joseph again as an example. Had he not suffered evil at the hands of his brethren, he would never have become the source of such incalculable blessing to others. Had he never suffered from the sin and lies of Potiphar's wife, his rise to be prime minister of Egypt would, in all probability, have been impossible. Had the chief cupbearer remembered his promise to Joseph earlier than he did, there is little likelihood that Joseph would have been at hand to play such a major role in the plight of the ancient near-east. *God's timing was perfect*. He not only held his servant back for the opportunity he had planned; he fashioned his experience and character to make him his instrument in the crisis.

Is such a God not entirely worthy of your trust and patient waiting on his will? It would be a denial of his grace to refuse him in the light of his credentials.

What then must we do, as we wait for him? We have suggested already that waiting in Scripture does not mean idly standing by. It is not a matter of resignation, but of commitment to the will of God. But what are we to do when we do not know what God wants us to do? What are we to do while we wait for the divine timetable to run its course? The answer of biblical precept and illustration is one. *Do your duty; live in the light God has already given you.* By walking in it you will find that God will make the future path clear – 'The path of the righteous is like the first gleam of dawn, shining ever brighter till the full light of day' (Prov. 4:18). This was the way our Master went. When his time had not yet come, when he was being held in and yet held back in connection with the baptism of the cross (Lk. 12:50), he walked in the light God had given him. The day came when the climax of his obedience was expressed in the acknowledgment of God's perfect will: 'not my will, but yours be done' (Lk. 22:42). He has given us the perfect example, that we should walk in his steps (1 Pet. 2:21).

> Wait for the Lord;
> be strong and take heart
> and wait for the Lord.

> Psalm 27:14

Blest is the man, O God,
That stays himself on Thee;
Who waits for Thy salvation, Lord,
Shall Thy salvation see.

When we in darkness walk,
Nor feel the heavenly flame,
Then is the time to trust our God,
And rest upon his Name.

Soon shall our doubts and fears
Subside at His control;
His lovingkindness shall break through
The midnight of the soul.

His grace will to the end
Stronger and brighter shine;
Nor present things, nor things to come,
Shall quench the light divine.

Augustus Montague Toplady

9: *He Leads Me*

We introduced ourselves to our consideration of the biblical teaching on God's guidance by making reference to the twenty-third Psalm. There is no more appropriate section of Scripture with which to draw our study to a conclusion. In so many ways it is to the Old Testament what the Lord's Prayer is to the New Testament – a summary of all the dimensions of the life of the Spirit. Furthermore, its whole ethos is that of the guiding and leading hand of the Lord. *He is our Shepherd.*

Psalm 23 is also *the voice of experience*. Just when David wrote these words may be a matter for conjecture. It is sometimes assumed, because of the shepherd metaphor, that they must have been composed when he was a youngster. But there are several reasons for believing that the experience which these lines record are more appropriate to a later period of David's life. After all, he knew then what it meant to be restored (v.3). In the last analysis, the psalm is not about being a shepherd. It is not meant to teach us animal husbandry. It is about God, and is intended to teach us about his ways.

So perfect is this part of Scripture that there seem to be almost endless ways in which the psalm can be expounded. For our present purposes, there are *six discoveries of personal experience* which merit our attention.

God supplies his people's needs (v.1). 'I shall not want'; 'I shall lack nothing'. David describes the perfection of the shepherd's care for his flock, making them lie down in *green* pastures, leading them beside quiet waters. He provides nourishment and rest for them. The sheep are his responsibility. The corresponding assurance for David is that God's grace will always be sufficient for every need he has. It will appear at the time of the Shepherd's wise appointment. Of course, when we arrive in green pastures, our natural tendency is to settle down. But the Shepherd-Saviour is wiser than his sheep. He will keep leading them on. He will maintain in their lives those rhythms of experience which are necessary for the production of Christian character and spiritual growth.

Can the wonder of this assurance be exaggerated? When the help I need, the rest for which I long in the will of God, seems to be so far away, does it not mean much to me to know that the One who is guiding me is perfect in wisdom *and* has perfect experience? He knows my needs before I ask him. He has plummeted the depths of each human need and tasted it from within our frail flesh. The glory of his ministry is not just that we have a shepherd. It is that he, Christ, is my Shepherd!

God restores his people (v.3). He restores my soul. There are three shadows cast across David's experience. Most familiar is the valley of the shadow of death. There is also the shadow of the presence of his enemies (v.5). But here he speaks of *the shadow of the past*. It is to his own failure that he is pointing; to the sins which made him cry in the great Psalm of Guidance, 'Remember not the sins of my youth and my rebellious ways . . . For the sake of your name, O Lord, forgive my iniquity, though it is great' (Ps. 25:7, 11). David never forgets the remnants of indwelling sin in his life which could so easily cause the Lord to turn his face from him, or cause himself to rebel against his Shepherd's clear direction. He owes obedience to him because he has been restored. He is a grateful member of the flock.

Many Christians need to learn David's lesson. Stumbling in the Christian life is not a final disqualification. God is merciful and forgiving. He is not willing that we should perish. He waits to bless us and save us, as we have seen (Is. 30:18). He longs to restore us when we stumble, fall and sin.

Think of the parable which Jesus told. The shepherd has a flock of one hundred sheep. One is lost. What does he do? Does he say: 'It has had all the provision I have made, and ungratefully rebelled. Let it be'? On the contrary, he leaves the comfort of his home; he leaves his other sheep in the fold. He pursues his lost sheep 'until he finds it' (Lk. 15:4). Then he brings it home 'joyfully', not *grudgingly* ('wretched beast, ungrateful creature!'), but *lovingly* 'on his shoulders'. There is no burden too great for the good shepherd to bear. He will give his life for the sheep. Indeed, our Good Shepherd has done so (Jn. 10:11, 17–18).

When you have strayed, and failed, you must return in penitence and faith. You may need to be *brought back*. Christ has made provision even for that. The names of his flock are all engraved on the shoulders and heart of the Shepherd-Priest of the new Israel (cf. Ex. 28:9–21). He is willing and able to restore you.

Peter's experience of this was the vital factor which equipped him to be not only a fisher of men, but a shepherd of God's flock. Think of his sin and failure!

Yet he was able, through restoring grace personally experienced, to say:

> And the God of grace, who called you to his eternal glory in Christ, after you have suffered a little while, will himself restore you and make you strong, firm and steadfast. To him be the power for ever and ever. Amen.

1 Peter 5:10

David – restored! Peter – restored! You may also be restored to the will of God.

God leads his people (v. 3). For the sake of his own name he guides us in paths of righteousness. Here is the heart of the matter, and it is expressed in a significant manner. *He* guides.

We have already seen that guidance is not so much something God *gives to us*, as something he *does for us*. His will is to take us in the paths of right living. We can leave the providential ordering to him. He calls us to follow behind him in the paths which are marked by righteousness. That is why we have found it necessary to lay so much emphasis on the place of the Bible in coming to know and obey the will of God. Its great purpose is to teach us, to introduce us to the character of God in its great doctrines, to work on our characters so that we may be trained in righteousness (2 Tim. 3:16). This is our equipment for doing the will of God.

Like the good shepherd, Jesus has gone before us; we have but to follow his footsteps (1 Pet. 2:21). He has pioneered the way of obedience through the undergrowth of this fallen world. It can never be so difficult for us to walk in the paths of righteousness as it was for him.

Only in worthy walking do we follow in the paths of

righteousness. That is where Christ leads us. Are you wandering, or following?

God protects his people (v.4). He guides us in the paths of righteousness, not necessarily the paths of ease, tranquillity or safety, by this world's standards. David had discovered that there were times when the paths of righteousness traversed dark and difficult terrain. He had walked 'through the valley of deep darkness', 'dark as death' (N.E.B.).

Doubtless our traditional understanding of these words is correct. The greatest shadow for most of us, the deepest valley through which we walk, is that of death – or the shadow of another's death. But David's words probably have a wider reference, for all trials cast shadows on our lives. God has not promised to guide us into fields of unperturbed immunity. Tribulation *works* something into the Christian's character, and so it too is used by God (Rom. 5:3).

God does promise us protection, however, when we walk in his will. We may not be safe, in the judgment of others. But there is no other safety for the Christian than in the will of God. For there alone has he promised to stand beside us. There alone will his rod and staff bring comforting, strengthening protection.

Sometimes for the Christian, too, life falls apart in his hands. Yes, even when he has been utterly obedient to his Lord. Paul found this, towards the end of his life. 'At my first defence', he writes to Timothy from his Roman prison, 'no one came to my support, but everyone deserted me.' To think that the mighty apostle, facing his great hour of crisis, should be reduced to such loneliness! How could he still believe in the guidance of God? 'But,' he says, 'the Lord stood at my side and gave me strength . . . and I was delivered from the lion's mouth. The Lord will rescue me from every evil attack and will bring me safely to his heavenly kingdom' (2 Tim. 4:16–18). Yes, he has promised never to leave us and never to forsake us!

God richly blesses his people (v.5). He prepares a feast for us in the presence of our enemies! He fills our cup to overflowing! How reminiscent of John Newton's words:

> *With salvation's walls surrounded*
> *Thou may'st smile at all thy foes.*

Our Chief Shepherd is a great encourager of his people as they walk in obedience to his will. He is full of surprises. Pursued by enemies, beaten down by failure, struggling to do his will – we find that he may lead us into a clearing and make joy abound in our hearts, while, for a season, he keeps all our foes at bay. He brings us to the banquet hall and raises over us the banner of his love (Song of Songs 2:4).

What has he promised to the obedient? Two words from Christ's lips will be sufficient for us:

No one who has left home or wife or brothers or parents or children for the sake of the kingdom of God will fail to receive many times as much in this age and, in the age to come, eternal life.

Luke 18:29–30

Whoever has my commands and obeys them, he is the one who loves me. He who loves me will be loved by my Father, *and I too will love him and show myself to him.* If anyone loves me, he will obey my teaching. *My Father will love him, and we will come to him and make our home with him.*

John 14:21, 23–4

God perseveres to the end with his people (v.6). His goodness and love will follow us all our days. This is blessing indeed. But David's words are stronger than most translations suggest. He uses the word 'pursue'. It is the kind of word which might have been used to describe sheepdogs pursuing the sheep into the safety of the fold.

God has two sheepdogs: Goodness and Mercy. He sends them to us from his throne of grace, sometimes to bark at us, to badger us; sometimes to woo us by persuading us that his will is good and perfect for our lives. He will not give up until his goodness and mercy have followed us home to his eternal glory.

This is why the Shepherd himself came. It is out of his death that goodness and mercy are purchased for the sheep. It is because of his sacrifice that God will never cease pursuing his children, persevering with them, until the likeness of Christ's obedience begins to radiate from their lives.

Is this not so? Has he ever failed? Have not those Christians who have been led through the darkest of all valleys been the very ones who have confessed that his goodness and mercy have followed them *all their days*? Is it not true that the eye of obedient faith can see what the eye of sight might too readily overlook?

Perhaps as you come to the end of these pages, God has been sending out his sheepdogs to pursue you – one of his straggling sheep. Do you not see that only in his will can you ever find the glory of God and the joy for which he created you? Will you not respond, and begin again to walk in his ways? For the day is coming when the sheepdogs will be called home. The Shepherd himself will appear (1 Pet. 5:4). We will no longer need the counsel of under-shepherds, summoning us to know the Lord and his will. We shall all know the Lord. There will be one flock. There will be one Shepherd—

Never again will they hunger;
 never again will they thirst.
The sun will not beat upon them,
 nor any scorching heat.
For the Lamb at the centre of the throne
 will be their shepherd;
he will lead them to springs of living water.

       Revelation 7:16–17

Far off I see the goal;
 O Saviour, guide me;
I feel my strength is small;
 Be Thou beside me:
With vision ever clear,
With love that conquers fear,
And grace to persevere,
 O Lord, provide me.

Whene'er Thy way seems strange,
 Go Thou before me;
And, lest my heart should change,
 O Lord, watch o'er me;
But should my faith prove frail,
And I through blindness fail,
O let Thy grace prevail,
 And still restore me.

Should earthly pleasures wane,
  And joy forsake me,
If lonely hours of pain
  At length o'ertake me,
My hand in Thine hold fast
Till sorrow be o'erpast,
And gentle death at last
  For heaven awake me.

There with the ransomed throng
  Who praise for ever
The love that made them strong
  To serve for ever,
I too would see Thy face,
Thy finished work retrace,
And magnify Thy grace,
Redeemed for ever.

Robert Rowland Roberts

Further Reading on the Subject of Guidance

Oliver R. Barclay: *Guidance* (Inter-Varsity Press).

Sinclair B. Ferguson: *Add to your Faith*, ch. 5 (Pickering & Inglis).

John Flavel: *The Mystery of Providence* (Banner of Truth).

John Murray: *Collected Writings*, vol. 1, ch. 26 (Banner of Truth).

James I. Packer: *Knowing God*, ch. 9, 10, 20 (Hodder & Stoughton).